THE INTEGRITY OF MISSION

THE INTEGRITY OF
MISSION

THE INNER LIFE AND OUTREACH
OF THE CHURCH

ORLANDO E. COSTAS

Published in San Francisco by

HARPER & ROW, PUBLISHERS

New York/Hagerstown/San Francisco/London

To
Johannes Verkuyl,
friend and teacher,
missionary and missiologist,
in recognition of his sacrificial
service to the Christian mission
throughout a long and distinguished
career in Indonesia and the Netherlands,
and for his contribution to the inner
life and outreach of the church in
other parts of the world.

FIRST EDITION

Designed by Paul Quin

Library of Congress Cataloging in Publication Data
Costas, Orlando E
  The integrity of mission.
  Bibliography: p. 108
  Includes index.
  1. Missions—Theory—Addresses, essays, lectures.
2. Missions—Addresses, essays, lectures. I. Title.
BV2063.C66   266'.001   79–1759
ISBN 0–06–061586–9

79 80 81 82 83 10 9 8 7 6 5 4 3 2 1

CONTENTS

ACKNOWLEDGMENTS

Like most authors, I owe many thanks to friends and colleagues. To some, for making direct contributions to my thinking at one stage or another in the process of preparing the manuscript. To others, for general encouragement and empathetic support. The latter group is extremely broad. Hence I will have to limit myself to the most obvious. The former is very specific. Following, a list of both.

The Board of Directors of the Latin American Evangelical Center for Pastoral Studies (CELEP), the colleagues who work out of the various offices (Brazil, Peru, Ecuador, Costa Rica and Mexico) and the friends, churches and agencies who make our ministry to pastors, churches and theological institutions throughout Latin America and the Caribbean possible.

The Rev. Dr. Thomas Hanks and Mr. Charles Troutman, friends and colleagues, for reading through the entire manuscript, offering numerous insights and helping me to make a smoother use of an undoubtedly beautiful but often tricky English language.

The many pastors, missionaries, lay leaders, theologues and theologians in many countries and several continents who not only provided the context for the production of these reflections but served as sounding boards for their rehearsal.

My devoted colleague and faithful wife, Mrs. Rose Feliciano Costas, for typing the manuscript several times and helping me to get past several conceptual and linguistic roadblocks.

To all of them my heartiest appreciation for helping me make this book possible. They are all exonerated for whatever "errors," "overstatements" or "heresies" the reader may discover throughout its pages.

Orlando E. Costas
Reformation Day 1978
San José, Costa Rica

FOREWORD

Integrity of Mission is a passionate plea for a biblically holistic approach to Christian mission.

For far too long, division has rent the contemporary church. While some of its representatives have been preoccupied with evangelism, others have focused on questions of social justice. While some have stressed the contemplative inward journey, others have championed an activist outward journey. While some have seen church growth largely in terms of numbers, others have disdained all dimensions of growth other than growth in costly discipleship.

Recent indications, however, suggest the possibility of significant convergence. The Chicago Declaration of Evangelical Social Concern and the section on Social Responsibility from the Lausanne Covenant demonstrate that a renewed concern for social justice is emerging in evangelical circles. The Fifth Assembly of the World Council of Churches in Nairobi issued a new call for evangelism. The pilgrimages of numerous individuals reflect a similar transition to increased social concern. When I travel, I meet evangelical Christians who have recently developed a vigorous concern for social justice as well as mainline Christians who discovered at the end of the activist 1960s that they needed a deeper biblical foundation to sustain their work for peace and justice. Certainly one dare not claim that a consensus has emerged. The battle for a faithful definition of Christian mission continues. But some significant unity in the next decade is a realistic possibility.

If that happens, it will be due in significant measure to the work of a new generation of evangelical theologians/missiologists from the Third World, including Orlando Costas. Daily confrontation with the agony of poverty and injustice precludes neglect of the scriptural summons to do justice. But that in no way entails abandoning the evangelistic task.

What Costas refuses to tolerate is onesidedness of any sort. In Chapter 1 (Mission as Proclamation), he insists on the centrality of verbal proclamation and personal decision, but also demands fundamentally transformed life-styles whose deeds give witness to the Good News. In Chapter 4 (Mission as Integral Growth), he reflects appreciation for church growth analysis and insists that God desires numerical growth, but also demands growth in radical discipleship that transforms the social order. He includes socio-economic liberation as a central dimension of the church's mission, but places equal emphasis on worship. "Liturgy without mission is like a river without a spring. Mission without worship is like a river without a sea. Both are necessary."

Several key theological themes are central to Costas's plea for a biblically holistic approach. Costas insists—rightly I believe—that faithful evangelistic proclamation today must return to Jesus' announcement of the Good News of the Kingdom. It is surely startling that the segment of the church which most proudly claims adherence to biblical authority almost never presents the content of the Gospel in the way the Gospels constantly say Jesus did—i.e., as the Good News of the Kingdom. Crucial too is Costas's emphasis on the church as the new messianic community, already incarnating the values of Jesus' kingdom. A third theme, developed at length in an excursus on "The Gospel and the Poor," is the scriptural emphasis on God's special concern for the poor.

I recently talked with the head of a large evangelical agency about the important biblical teaching that God is on the side of the poor. "How," he asked in perplexed reflection, "could I study and then teach at evangelical colleges and seminaries and never become aware of this central biblical theme until this year?" How indeed! The scriptures have just as much to say about the fact that God is on the side of the poor as they do about the resurrection of Jesus. And yet evangelicals have insisted on belief in the resurrection of Jesus of Nazareth as a criterion of orthodoxy and largely neglected the fact that God is on the side of the poor. Knowing Jehovah is not, as some suggest, identical with seeking justice for the poor and oppressed, but they are certainly inseparable. We must confess that as evangelicals we have been far less orthodox than we thought.

Orlando Costas's previous books and articles have already demonstrated that he is a significant, creative, evangelical theologian. One can only hope and pray that his summons to holistic mission, renewed in *The Integrity of Mission*, will be heard by all segments of the church.

RONALD J. SIDER

Eastern Baptist Theological Seminary

INTRODUCTION

The word *mission* has become a controversial term in modern Christians' vocabulary. A Belgian Catholic theologian, Joseph Comblin, who has spent a greater part of the last twenty years in Latin America, has stated in a recent publication that "the theology of . . . mission is the central issue where the major controversies among Christians converge."[1] That is true not only among Roman Catholics, but also among Protestants. It reflects the situation not only in Latin America, but in North America and elsewhere around the world.

The roots of the problem are too long and complicated to trace here. Generally speaking, the problem is closely related to the fact that we wear different "eye glasses." We view reality from different angles. These glasses have been colored by our experience, life-situation and intellectual formation, all of which force us to see things in particular ways. We sense issues and priorities differently.

The crucial problem in mission today is whether we can overcome our particularities, get a glimpse of its totality, and maintain its integrity; or in other words, whether we can repossess earnestly and urgently the biblical vision of a holistic mission, carried out faithfully and consistently in the crossroads of life. We are experiencing a crisis of wholeness and integrity. The fundamental missiological question before the Christian church is not whether mission should be conceived of as vertical, horizontal, or both; not whether it should be thought of either as spiritual and personal, or material and social; nor whether we should emphasize in our practice one aspect or another. It is rather whether we can recover its wholeness and efficacy, whether we can see it as a whole and live up to its global objectives.

This problem has been of particular concern in my theological reflection. In *The Church and Its Mission* (1974), my concern was to explore the place of the church in God's mission in the light of its nature and growth, along with the leading tensions in the church's present-day involvement in mission. I advocated a comprehensive approach to mission that would make clear beyond the shadow of a doubt the wholeness of the gospel. In *Theology of the Crossroads*, I pursued the same theme in reference to the formal discipline of missiology in the context of Latin American Protestantism. In that work I defined missiology as a holistic field of study: a critical and contextual reflection in the tumultuous crossroads of life. I stated that "missiology is concerned not just with the specificity of mission (the . . . sharing of the gospel with the world and its concrete responses), but with its overall setting, its context and environment. . . . [This] involves the entire life of the church."[2]

In the present work I seek to analyze further, though in a more popular form, the various aspects that make up the church's mission-in-life. I want to focus on the various dimensions of its one-world-mission as they become operative in everyday life. My purpose is a modest one: to look at the Christian world mission as a unitary, indivisible whole, in the hope of generating a wider vision and stimulating a more effective missional involvement. In comparison with my previous works this one popularizes and concretizes—and I hope deepens—my quest for an integral understanding of mission that will enable the church to snap out of its inward-looking syndrome, its defeatist minority complex and its polarized missiological outlook. We need to get on with the job that needs to be done. It is a comprehensive task, affecting both the inner life and outreach of the church, with evangelistic, educational, administrative, ethical, diaconal and liturgical dimensions.

The essays that follow have originated in various church meetings. Four of them (chapters I, II, V and VI) were originally delivered at the Global Mission Conference of the Presbyterian Church in the U.S. in Montreat, North Carolina, in August 1977. One (chapter IV) initially was given as a series of inspirational messages at a National Pastors' Conference in Dalat, Vietnam, in January 1975 and was repeated at the American Baptist Conference on Church Growth in Louisville, Kentucky, in September 1977, and at the Annual Conference for Missionaries on Furlough of the Reformed Church in America in Crete, Illinois, in July 1978. It has been revised for publication. Chapter III[3] was originally delivered, along with chapters I and II, at a "Conference on The Renewal of Enthusiasm in Preaching" for pastors of the Rocky Mountain States under the auspices of Central Baptist Theological Seminary, the American Baptist Churches of the Rocky Mountains and its Board of National Ministries in Denver, Colorado, in March 1978.

Thus each chapter has been prepared with particular audiences in mind: pastors and church leaders primarily from North American mainline Protestant churches. But since I write both as an evangelical and a mainline Protestant, what I have to say should also be applicable to conservative evangelicals from other denominations. As a Latin American I write from a minority ecclesial context and a Catholic cultural milieu. It should be said, therefore, that though these essays have been written primarily for Protestants what I have to say has been positively enriched by my daily contact with Roman Catholic theologians, lay members and clergy. By the same token, the fact that the crisis of mission is as much a reality among Roman Catholics as among Protestants, as witnessed by the statement from Joseph Comblin quoted above, what I have to say should be equally relevant to Catholics.

This collection of essays is dedicated to a Dutch missiologist who has practiced and taught its content throughout a long and distinguished career. It is my modest way of paying tribute to a man who has not only been a source of inspiration to me personally, but a wise pastor and teacher and a warm friend—in this (1978) the year of his retirement from the chair of mission and evangelism at the Free (Reformed) University of Amsterdam in the Netherlands.

CHAPTER I

MISSION AS PROCLAMATION

The Christian faith is grounded in God's Word. That Word is the process by which God makes himself known and transmits his will to humankind. The Bible is the faithful record of that process; it tells us not only *how* God communicates with women, men and children, but also *what* he says.[1]

That Word has been entrusted to the church in order that it might transmit it to the world. The apostle Paul says that the Word of Scripture has been given in order that we might find "salvation through faith in Christ Jesus" (2 Tim. 3:15).* Thus, the Word of the gospel is the nutshell of God's revelation. It is why Paul states emphatically in Rom. 10:17 that "faith comes from what is heard, and what is heard comes by the preaching of Christ," that is, by the "good news" that Christ has brought to the world. A chief task of the church, therefore, is to proclaim the gospel.

This is clearly underscored in the oldest of the four Gospels. In the first chapter of the Gospel of Mark we read:

*Biblical quotations in this book, unless otherwise noted, are from the Revised Standard Version of the Bible, copyrighted 1946, 1952, © 1971, 1973.

The beginning of the gospel of Jesus Christ, the Son of God. As it is written in Isaiah the prophet, "Behold, I send my messenger before thy face, who shall prepare thy way; the voice of one crying in the wilderness: Prepare the way of the Lord, make his paths straight."

John the baptizer appeared in the wilderness, preaching a baptism of repentance for the forgiveness of sins. . . .

Now after John was arrested, Jesus came into Galilee, preaching the gospel of God. . . . (Mark 1:1–4; 14)

Both John and Jesus were "sent ones." They were emissaries.[2] John was sent to prepare the way for Jesus, who was, in turn, sent to fulfill God's mission in history. It is significant that both came "preaching."

To preach is to herald a message. A preacher is an envoy, sent to proclaim a message on God's behalf. Many have wrongly associated this with sermonizing, *i.e.*, with the formal oral religious discourses prepared by professional clergy persons and delivered during worship services. But preaching is neither bound to a set form nor to the particular realm of the religious professional. Proclamation is a dynamic act that affects the whole life of the emissary. It is an ongoing, ceaseless task. It lies at the center of the mission which God has entrusted to his people.

A basic aspect of Jesus' own mission was proclamation.[3] Since he is the ground and model for ours, we need to understand the nature of his message.

PROCLAIMING GOD'S NAME

The Mark passage outlines several characteristics of the message Jesus came proclaiming. First of all, Jesus' proclamation was grounded in God. He came preaching "the gospel of God." That is, he came announcing good news from God. This message is no mere conceptual package which can be treated as an absolute entity. In the biblical tradition God's Word is always linked with his personality. To proclaim a message from God is to affirm God's name, or God himself, since his name is a designation of himself.[4]

This God whom Jesus came proclaiming was no stranger to

his largely Jewish audiences. By tradition they had come to recognize him as "the first" and "the last"; they had learned that before and besides him there was no other god. In light of his "before allness," they were also aware that he held all persons accountable. As Paul states in his Epistle to the Romans (a document that also expounds "the gospel of God" and that, according to New Testament scholars, is highly influential on the Gospel of Mark):

> . . . on the day of wrath . . . God's righteous judgment will be revealed . . . [and] he will render to every man according to his works. . . . All who have sinned without the law will also perish without the law, and all who sinned under the law will be judged by the law. . . . on that day when . . . God judges the secrets of men . . . . (Rom. 2:5, 6, 12, 16)

The fact of God's sovereignty, and therefore of his forthcoming judgment, is hammered out time and again in the prophetic literature of the Old Testament. Thus John the Baptist, considered the last of the prophets of the old dispensation, came preaching a message of judgment:

> You brood of vipers! Who warned you to flee from the wrath to come? Bear fruits that befit repentance, and do not begin to say to yourselves, 'We have Abraham as our Father'; for I tell you, God is able from these stones to raise up children to Abraham. Even now the axe is laid to the root of the trees; every tree therefore that does not bear good fruit is cut down and thrown into the fire. (Lk. 3:7–9)

This God who calls every man, woman and child to accountability, who is *before* and *above* all, is also God *for* all. He is the God of love who has given himself to the human race in creation and providence, who gave his name to an insignificant people and through his "covenant" consecrated them to be "a light to the nations." He has willed "to open" blind eyes and to bring them "out of darkness into his marvelous light."[5]

Hence, the message of John the Baptist cannot be seen merely as a word of judgment. John came proclaiming the way of repentance as well as the imminence of the wrath of God. He came "crying in the wilderness" (the place of solitude and captivity), announcing a "new exodus," which demanded preparation, a change of attitudes and values, the beginning of a new way of life.

Prepare the way of the Lord,
make his paths straight.
Every valley shall be filled,
and every mountain and hill shall be brought low,
and the crooked shall be made straight,
and the rough ways shall be made smooth;
and all flesh shall see the salvation of God. (Lk. 3:4–6)

The God of the gospel is sovereign and merciful. "He is not far from each one of us" (Acts 17:27). His presence in the world is witnessed to by nature, history, our personal consciousness and the many special ways by which he has chosen to make himself known to men and women everywhere. He is present in the rain that falls on our ground, the sun that shines on our faces and the moon that lights our path. He is present in the exercise of our multiple personal, cultural and social gifts. And particularly he is present in the sufferings of the orphan and the widow, the hungry and the thirsty, the prisoner, the foreigner and the persecuted. Paul says, "In him we live and move and have our being" (Acts 17:28).

These three aspects of God ("before," "for" and "in" all)[6] find their most dramatic manifestation in Jesus of Nazareth. He embodied uniquely and supremely God's authority and freedom, his love and compassion and the reality of his presence in human history. This fact is underscored in the Prologue of John's Gospel: the Word, which was from the beginning, through whom everything was made, in whom was life and who "was the light of men," became flesh in Jesus of Nazareth. He "dwelt among us" and revealed God's truth and grace.[7]

In saying that Jesus came proclaiming "the gospel of God," Mark is telling us that Jesus was himself God's good news. It is Mark's way of expressing what other writers of the New Testament affirm, namely, that Jesus was God's final word to humankind, the fulfillment of "all the promises of God," the awaited savior, the faithful representative of the Father, whom he has made "both Lord and Christ." A transition can thus be witnessed in the New Testament from the name of God to the name of Jesus. Jesus, says Peter, is the name that the Father has given for our salvation. "And there is salvation in no one else, for there is no other name under heaven given among men by which we must be saved" (Acts 4:12).

If in the Old Testament the people of God had as a fundamental task the proclamation of the name of *Yahweh* among the nations, in the New Testament that task becomes explicit in the proclamation of the name of Jesus. Yet, as the National Council of Churches in the USA pointed out in 1976 in its "Policy Statement on Evangelism," it is a fact that in our day many Christians and churches "seem strangely bound by a reluctance to name the Name of Jesus as Lord and Saviour."[8] The reasons for such reluctance are varied. Perhaps one of the strongest is the tremendous sensitivity that some Christians and churches have developed about the futility of words. As a friend said to me once: "The world is tired of words. It wants to see, not hear." Thus, the trend has been to "implicitate" rather than "explicitate," to show rather than tell, to bear witness by sign rather than through words.

Yet the importance of the tangible and visible in the communication of the gospel cannot be denied. But as Mortimer Arias reminded the delegates at the WCC Assembly in Nairobi, "The New Testament proclamation unites sign and word."[9] Therefore it is neither biblical nor theologically sound to omit the explicitation, the verbalization, of the name of Jesus, not even if there is an aversion against words. Present-day Christians would do well to heed the word Yahweh to the prophet Ezekiel:

> "Son of man, I send you to the people of Israel, to a nation of rebels . . . you shall say to them, 'Thus says the Lord God.' And whether they hear or refuse to hear . . . they will know that there has been a prophet among them." (Ezek. 2:3–5)

Unlike Ezekiel, we have not been sent to Israel to deliver a message of judgment. But we have been sent to proclaim the Word which God has spoken in Christ to the whole creation, no matter whether it hears or refuses to hear.

PROCLAIMING GOD'S KINGDOM

The proclamation of God's name in Jesus' ministry was qualified by the announcement of God's kingdom. Mark tells us that "Jesus came . . . preaching the gospel of God, . . . saying, 'The time is fulfilled, and the kingdom of God is at hand' " (Mk. 1:14–15). As in the Old Testament, where the prophetic proclamation of God's name finds concrete expression in his reign over the nations, and especially in the midst of Israel, so in the New Testament the gospel of God finds its most concrete reference to Jesus' announcement of the kingdom.

The kingdom which Jesus proclaimed, however, cannot be viewed apart from his life and ministry. Just as God's name became flesh in the name of Jesus, so Jesus embodies the presence of God's kingdom. With the appearance of Jesus, the kingdom of God has drawn near, *i.e.*, it has come within the reach of everyone. A more concrete, specific and personal understanding of the kingdom is now made possible. In Jesus' life and ministry God discloses the content of his kingdom far more clearly, comprehensively and deeply than in the life and history of Israel. Of the many aspects of this disclosure that can be underscored, two stand out.

The kingdom is an indication of God's transforming presence in history. It is not just the symbol of God's sovereignty, signified, as in the Old Testament, by his mighty deeds among the nations and in Israel. It is that, of course, but much more. It is a symbol of God's transforming power, of his determination to make "all things new" (Rev. 21:5). The kingdom of God stands for a new order of life: the new humanity and the new creation which have become possible through the death and resurrection of Jesus.[10] This new order includes reconciliation with God, neighbor and nature, and, therefore, participation in a new world. It involves freedom from the power of sin and death, and, consequently, the strength to live for God and humanity. It encompasses the hope of a more just and peaceful moral order, and thus it is a call to vital engagement in the historical struggles for justice and peace.

This transforming power is also disclosed as an eschatological reality. It is the beginning of the end. As such, it awaits the final consummation of history. It is a force that anticipates the final redemption, which is made possible by the work of the Holy Spirit[11] and which is borne witness to by what the Gospels call "the signs of the kingdom." These are deeds that point beyond themselves to the ultimate fulfillment of God's purpose. "The kingdom of which the New Testament speaks," says J. Verkuyl, has an incomparable depth and richness. It has dimensions which embrace heaven and earth, world history and the cosmos (cf. Colossians and Ephesians). The kingdom of God is the new order, which began in Christ and which will be completed by Him, wherein all relationships will be put right, and not only that between God and man but also those between people, nations, sexes, generations and races, and that between man and nature. It is this of which the prophets of Israel speak. This is the meaning of the visions in the book of Revelation. And it is this of which the apostles testify when they speak of looking forward to new heavens and a new earth where justice dwells (2 Pet. 3:13).[12]

Regrettably, many Christians give very little emphasis to the message of the kingdom. They either push it to a far future or wrongly suppose that it was overcome as a central concern of the gospel by our Lord's death and resurrection. They forget that the four New Testament Gospels are post-Easter interpretations of Jesus' life and ministry, that the Gospels see the kingdom as both present and future and that this is a central theme of the preaching of the early church—as the Book of Acts, Hebrews, 1 Peter and Revelation clearly show.

I come from a spiritual tradition (Protestant evangelicalism) which has stressed the proclamation of the gospel, but has, by and large, deemphasized the concept of the kingdom. Michael Green, speaking at the Lausanne International Congress on World Evangelization (1974), underscored this tremendous flaw in evangelical theology. He said that as evangelicals "We tend to isolate what we call the Gospel from what Jesus called the kingdom of God." Then, referring to the Congress, he asked:

> How much have we heard here about the kingdom of God? Not much. It is not our language. But it was Jesus' prime concern. He came to show that God's kingly rule had broken into our world: it no longer lay entirely in the future, but was partly realized in him and those who followed him. The Good News of the kingdom was both preached by Jesus and embodied by him . . . So it must be with us.[13]

We have stressed so much the otherness of the kingdom that we have forgotten its nearness. Jesus spoke of the kingdom not only as a transcendent and future reality, but also as immanent and present: "behold, the kingdom of God is in the midst of you" (Lk. 17:21). Jesus himself was the kingdom! Anyone who believed in him experienced the kingdom. That is why John referred to the kingdom as "eternal life" and then went on to define it as knowledge of the one true God and Jesus Christ whom he had sent (Jn. 17:3).

Whoever believes in Jesus Christ knows him personally, is in fellowship with the Father and has entered the kingdom. Therefore, the church, which is *not* the kingdom, is nevertheless its most *visible expression* and its most *faithful interpreter* in our age. It is the body of Christ. As the community of believers from all times and places, the church both *embodies* the kingdom in its life and *witnesses* to its presence and future in its mission.

We need to repossess the concept of the kingdom as the new reality that the gospel announces. We need to proclaim it in words and deeds—affirming it with our mouths and embodying it in our lives. Otherwise we drive a wedge between Jesus and the new age he inaugurated, between the gospel and the reality it proclaims, between the Word and its sign. Like Phillip in Samaria; we need to preach "good news about the kingdom of God and the name of Jesus Christ" (Acts 8:12).

PROCLAIMING GOD'S MOMENT

Jesus' proclamation was characterized also by the summons to decision. The precise moment, the appointed time, the hour of salvation has come to pass. Therefore, "repent and believe in the gospel."

The gospel represents, on the one hand, God's moment of grace: his invitation to women and men to come to terms with their creator and discover their true humanity. No neutrality is allowed. One must choose whether or not to accept God's offer of grace. On the other hand, the gospel *demands* a change of values and attitudes as a fundamental condition for participation in the life of the kingdom. Jesus said, "unless you turn and become like children, you will never enter the kingdom of heaven" (Mt. 18:3).

The call to conversion is thus an invitation and a demand. It is an invitation to participate in the new humanity which God is realizing through Jesus Christ and the power of his Spirit. But it is also a demand for total commitment to God and neighbor. No half way is possible. One must repent, change his or her mind, abandon the old order of life, accept a new perspective on reality and adopt a new lifestyle. And one must believe in the good news of God—that is, trust in, adhere to and accept what God has done in his Son. No area of life may be left out. The whole of it must come under Jesus Christ's lordship.

Conversion is not a static, once-for-all, private event. To be sure, it has a profoundly personal dimension and marks a distinct moment in the history of the converted individual. But it is also an ongoing process.

The call to conversion in Jesus' preaching was an invitation to a journey—a journey into the mystery of the kingdom of God, which leads from one challenge to another. Initiation in this journey plunges us into an adventure where we are confronted with ever new decisions, ever new turning points, ever new fulfillments and ever new promises. This will continue until the kingdom's consummation at the return of Christ. Our plunge confronts us, moreover, with the need to return repeatedly to the fundamental point of reference and to engage in ever new routings. The fundamental point of reference (that initial encounter with God, the beginning of the journey), however, is not a static, fixed point, but a foundational signpost that accompanies the individual throughout the journey, similar to the traveling tabernacle in the Old Testament or the *anamnesis* (remembrance) that the children of Israel engaged in year after year in the Passover. A living again, at whatever point of their pilgrimage, of the Passover celebration.

On certain occasions I have referred to my own conversion as a complex experience, encompassing a personal religious conversion to Christ, a cultural conversion to Puerto Rico and Latin America and a sociopolitical conversion to the world, particularly the world of the poor.[14] These conversion experiences are not divorced but are interrelated. Thus the conversion to Christ is foundational, the cultural a consequence of my new identity in Christ and the sociopolitical an outgrowth of my calling as a follower of the man Christ-Jesus, who identified himself with the destitute of the earth. Yet these interrelated experiences are not all the turnings which I will experience in the course of my spiritual pilgrimage. I live, therefore, in a sphere of continuous transformations (2 Cor. 3:18).

That this interpretation of conversion—as both a distinct moment and a continuous process—is biblically valid can be argued from the uses in the New Testament of the two key terms for conversion.

Epistrépho was the Greek word used most often by the Septuagint to translate the leading Old Testament term for repentance: *shub*.[15] It means to turn, bring back or return. *Epistrépho* is often used in relation to the turning of unbelievers (for the first time) to God from their sins.[16] But sometimes it is linked to erring believers who are brought back into a right relation with God.[17]

The other term often used in the New Testament is *metanoéo*. It means to change one's mind, often feeling regret, and "to adopt another view."[18] It is used both in the context of the call to forgiveness from sin and liberation from future judgment and in reference to the problem of apostasy inside the church.

Metanoéo is closely connected with *epistrépho*, as where Peter calls the multitude to "Repent . . . and turn again." It also appears in connection with *pisteuo*, which means to believe, or "to adhere, to trust or rely on." Thus Jesus summoned his hearers to "repent, and believe in the gospel" (Mk. 1:15).

These different words and their uses in Scripture underscore, at the very least, the fact that conversion entails a new allegiance, a new trust and a new life-commitment. This newness is, nevertheless, the beginning of a rather long journey and carries implicitly the seed of new turns.

Some might be tempted to argue that this latter aspect is more congruent with the concept of sanctification than of conversion. They would argue that it is too confusing when we use the same word to designate two different phenomena. "If everything is conversion, then nothing is conversion." Thus it would be better to call additional "turnings" in the life of believers *renewal* or even *revival*.

But that is just the problem. There does not seem to be any hard biblical or theological evidence for the neat, clear-cut distinction between conversion and sanctification that one finds in traditional Protestant Reformed theologies. On the contrary, sanctification seems to be implicit in conversion and conversion in sanctification. In fact, this tendency to separate conversion and sanctification may be blocking some contemporary Christians from coming to terms with the reality of their internal corruption and unbelief. It lets them hide comfortably behind an experience that occurred in the past. These Christians lose sight of the fact that one of the most crucial distinctives of the biblical doctrine of conversion is that it can be verified only in the concrete manifestation of a distinctive quality of life. It is not enough to say that one is converted; one must *live* a converted life! That is why the prophets of Israel reserved their strongest call to conversion to the people of Israel, because having believed in the living God they were often denying him in practice. That is why four out of the seven churches of Asia are exhorted to repent.

To limit conversion to the non-Christian would be, therefore, a disservice to the church. It would be an imposition of western logic—which thrives upon definitions and verbal distinctions, compartmentalizing reality—upon biblical thought. Biblical thought sees reality more holistically. It does not allow us to fall into comfortable positions and spiritual illusions. As Paul says to the Corinthians, "Therefore let anyone who thinks that he stands take heed lest he fall" (1 Cor. 10:12).

We are being assailed in the church today by two equally dangerous tendencies. On the one hand, we see an evangelistic aggressiveness so geared to "the outsider" that it limits the call to conversion to an initial moment of decision, divorcing it from all ethical demands. In such a perspective, the important thing is to get people to decide for Christ, to feel sorry about their past sins and to let Jesus handle it all from now on. That approach enables women and men to enter the kingdom without undue ethical obstacles. It liberates the church from having to worry about the fact that it is constantly threatened by sin and evil. It runs the risk of adopting values, attitudes and behavioral patterns that are contrary to the gospel, thereby placing the church in a state of functional if not actual unbelief. In other words, that approach lets the church begin to treat the problem of atheism (denial of God) only in reference to those who are outside its fellowship—that is, as a problem of non-Christians and not as a reality that affects Christians as well. We know, however, that some of the greatest atheists in our day are not outside but inside the church. Those individuals deny with their actions faith in the God of the living, who demands love, truth and righteousness from those who confess his name and orders them to depart from idols, deceit and immorality.

There are those, on the other hand, who seem to give little importance to the call to conversion. Somehow they have accommodated themselves to the more befitting, respectable, comfortable and less offensive religious practice of established Christianity. They have thus left the language of repentance, conversion and the new birth to so-called revivalistic organizations, far-out sects, fundamentalistic or conservative denominations. Meanwhile the joy and radiance of the gospel seem to be fading from their lives. Their missional involvement seems to be rapidly waning. Their life commitments seem to be becoming mechanistic. The pews of their congregations seem to be slowly dwindling as more and more parishioners, frustrated with shallow or formalistic religiosity, begin simply to drop out of sight, or turn to transcendental meditation groups, or join more spiritually committed churches.

If present-day Christianity is not to be reduced to a museum piece, a historically insignificant religion, a topic of the past, a corpse or a free-floating religious club, it will need to recover the urgency of proclaiming three things: the name of Jesus, the radical nature of God's kingdom and the call to repentance and faith. This is another way of saying that its pulpit (which is a central agency of its message and mission) will need to make *proclamation* a central aspect of its function. Its ministers and pastors will have to recover first the urgency of proclaiming the gospel and then the prophetic courage to preach conversion not only to those who are on the outside, but also to those who may be inside but nonetheless far from God's kingdom. Individual Christians, local churches, denominations and missionary agencies will need to heed the exhortation to the church at Ephesus: "Remember from what you have fallen, repent and do the works you did at first. If not, I will come to you and remove your lampstand from its place. . . . He who has an ear, let him hear what the Spirit says to the churches" (Rev. 2:5, 7).

CHAPTER II

MISSION
AS DISCIPLE-MAKING

One of the positive signs in the Christian church today is the reappearance of the biblical concept of discipleship. We see it in the emergence of Christian publications dedicated to the exploration of discipleship through new movements and programs. We see new emphasis on disciple-making as a fundamental dimension of the ministry of the Word. Undergirding this is the growing conviction that the proclamation of the gospel needs to be complemented by the making of disciples. Or, in other words, that ministry *in breadth* must be accompanied by ministry *in depth* if the ministry of the Word is to keep its biblical integrity and comprehensiveness.

The reappearance of the concept of disciple-making as a central thrust of Christian ministry is a rediscovery of a basic New Testament concern. It is no surprise that in the same chapter and book where we find one of the most succinct, yet forceful references to the proclamation of the gospel there is also an immediate reference to the ministry of teaching.

And passing along by the Sea of Galilee, he saw Simon and Andrew the brother of Simon casting a net in the sea; for they were fishermen. And Jesus said to them, "Follow me and I will make you become fishers of men." And immediately they left their nets and followed him. And going on a little farther, he saw James the son of Zebedee and John his brother, who were in their boat mending the nets. And immediately he called them; and they left their father Zebedee in the boat with the hired servants, and followed him. (Mk. 1:16–20)

Less we be tempted to reduce this task to a secondary stage, we should note that reference to this incident does not follow chronologically the preaching of Jesus referred to in Mk. 1:14–15. The latter is a summary statement of what Jesus did. The incident narrated in 1:16-20 is a unit of its own—a pericope which finds its parallels in the other Gospels. It refers to an incident that Mark inserts in this spot with a clear theological criterion: to signify a dimension of Jesus' ministry that must accompany and give concretion to the proclamation of the kingdom of God. The call to discipleship is a necessary correlation of the proclamation of the kingdom because it indicates a fundamental—indeed the most concrete—means by which the kingdom of God is manifested in history. It shows that at the heart of Jesus' preaching there was the idea of a community that would embody his life and carry on his mission.

What does it mean to make disciples? The call of the first apostles offers several specific guidelines.

FOLLOWING JESUS

To make disciples means, in the first place, to lead women and men to follow Jesus. "And Jesus said to them, 'Follow me and I will make you become fishers of men.' " The invitation to follow is significant since it is similar to the way the rabbis got their disciples. In the case of Jesus, it implied a life of commitment. It involved surrendering to his care one's life-ambitions, personal needs and group loyalties. It meant submission to a new discipline, adoption of a new lifestyle and incorporation into a new community. It confronted these four Galilean fishermen with a demand so profound that they would be able to appreciate its full implications only in the aftermath of the resurrection, and even then they would need the ongoing illumination of the Spirit for the rest of their lives.

Though Jesus' invitation to "follow" sounded similar to that of the rabbis of his day, it was, nevertheless, quite different. Juan Stam has listed seven basic differences between following Jesus and following the rabbis.

1. Following Jesus was by invitation only, whereas with the rabbis it was by request. The rabbinic disciples chose their teachers rather than the teachers choosing the disciples, as was the case with Jesus.

2. Becoming a disciple of Jesus involved a practical education that encompassed one's entire way of life. With the rabbis, it was purely intellectual, theoretical and abstract.

3. Jesus' invitation to follow was grounded on a personal relationship. That of the rabbis was basically doctrinal.

4. Following Jesus was a gift of grace. The disciple was not required to pay Jesus' salary. With the rabbis, it was in some sense a commercial enterprise, since their disciples were obligated to pay for their instruction.

5. The discipleship of Jesus demanded absolute commitment. The rabbis did not and could not make such a demand.

6. With Jesus, the life of discipleship was a communal reality; he and his disciples constituted a closely knit fellowship. With the rabbis, there was hardly any room for fellowship.

7. The discipleship of Jesus was permanent. The invitation was for life. No one could, therefore, expect to "graduate." In the case of the rabbis, it was a temporary learning program. The goal of the rabbinic disciples was to become rabbis themselves, once the training period was over, whereas with the disciples of Jesus they were expected to go on learning from, depending upon and serving their Master.[1]

Thus, although there were many similarities between Jesus and the rabbis, the contrasts were far greater. Little wonder that those who heard him "were astonished at his teaching, for he taught them as one who had authority, and not as the scribes" (Mk. 1:22).

To lead others to follow Jesus is not a mechanistic task of recruitment, where people are brought into an undemanding and thoughtless relationship. Neither is it an intellectual exercise, where others are convinced of the truth claims of the teachings of Jesus and are led to give intellectual assent to them. Following Jesus is not based on religious slogans, psychological tactics and evangelistic brainwashing. Nor is it grounded on the assimilation of complicated theological formulations.

Following and leading others to follow Jesus is a continuous process based on an effective personal relationship with him. It involves, of course, a basic understanding of who Jesus is, what he did and where he wants to guide us in life. It involves the development and exercise of effective methods of communication. But the key to this process of intake and output, of reception and transmission, is the authority and effective presence of Jesus himself in our lives.

Matthew's account of the Great Commission is helpful at this point.[2] It opens up with the affirmation of the authority that the risen Christ has been given and concludes with the promise of his presence until the end of the age. In between, lies the task of disciple-making, leading others to become one with him in baptism, teaching them to observe what he has commanded. Because Jesus has led the way, because he has authority to lead and command and makes himself present in the struggles of our life, we are able to lead others to follow him. This means that we ourselves are compelled to go all the way with him and teach others to do likewise. The promise of Jesus is ineffective if we do not constantly submit ourselves to his lordship. The disciples we make will turn out to be spurious, false, superficial and useless if we do not teach them to be continuously and unconditionally committed to Jesus' lifestyle.

Here lies a fundamental problem. The church has allowed itself to believe that making disciples is merely a quantitative task, *i.e.*, a numerical enterprise. It has assumed that the easier it makes it to follow Jesus, the more it adapts the gospel to the cultural situation, the more people will be able to be discipled. That false assumption has dominated not only the church's evangelistic practice, but also its way of conceiving the Christian life—so that the way *to* Christ has been softened, the life *in* Christ has been watered down. Dietrich Bonhoeffer called this "cheap grace."[3] René Padilla has labeled it "culture-Christianity."[4] Juan Luis Segundo has likened it to the massification of society.[5]

This reality may be witnessed everywhere in the church. Segundo, for example, argues that ever since Constantine, Christianity has been infested by the process of massification. He says that after Constantine it was made so easy to be a Christian that Christianity became devalued. He goes on to state that this is precisely what has happened in Latin America, where instead of a committed Christian church, there has emerged a massified Christianity. Bonhoeffer had western Europe in mind, and particularly the German situation, when he spoke of the cheapening of grace. René Padilla, however, while admitting the reality of "culture Christianity" around the world, has pointed out that the most influential form, the most dangerous for the cause of the gospel around the world today, is the one that has come to be identified with "the American Way of Life." North American sociologist David Moberg has described this phenomenon like this: "We have equated 'Americanism' with Christianity to such an extent that we are tempted to believe that people in other cultures must adopt American institutional patterns when they are converted. We are led through natural psychological processes to an unconscious belief that the essence of our American Way of Life is basically, if not entirely, Christian."[8]

The problem with this form of Christianity, which characterizes in one way or another the majority of churches and Christians in the USA, is not just the powerful influence it has had on the traditional "mission fields" around the world—how it has inhibited the gospel from taking root among those who have been evangelized. Even more important is what this "way of life" has done to the gospel itself—reducing it to "a conscience-soothing Jesus, with an unscandalous cross; an other-worldly kingdom; a private, inwardly, individualistically limited Holy Spirit; a pocket God; a spiritualized Bible" and a church that escapes from the gut issues of society.[7] It has conceived the goal of the gospel as "a happy, comfortable and successful life, obtainable through the forgiveness of an abstract sinfulness by faith in an unhistorical Christ." It has made possible "the 'conversion' of men and women without having to make any drastic changes in their lifestyles and worldviews," guaranteeing thereby "the preservation of the status quo and the immobility of the people of God."[8]

True Christian discipleship cannot be equated with such a

distorted gospel. Such a gospel can make only proselytes, false and spurious Christians, not true disciples of Jesus. The true disciple follows Jesus to the cross and is not ashamed to "bear the abuse he endured" (Heb. 13:13). Nor is he or she motivated by the vision of a "successful life." Rather the true disciple is moved by the desire to be a good and faithful servant of the kingdom.[9]

I know a former Dutch missionary who during the Indonesian struggle for independence decided to be faithful to the demands of the kingdom rather than stand by the imperialistic capriciousness of his own country. He felt that to be a true disciple of Jesus Christ at that time was to stand by the side of Indonesians in their just struggle against Dutch colonialism. This both disgraced and stigmatized him in the eyes of his government and Dutch compatriots, as well as resulted in excommunication by his church and mission board. Yet he decided to bear the abuse of the cross by standing in solidarity with Sukarno and the Indonesian people. Today, reinstituted into the fellowship of his church, he is not only held in high esteem by a new generation of Dutch citizens who abhor the colonial past of the Netherlands and the tragic consequences of Dutch Reformed constantinianism in places like South Africa, but he is also remembered by the Indonesian people as a missionary who stood by their side in their national ordeal.

This man was my professor. As I look into my present situation in Latin America, I cannot think of a more fitting person to guide me along in my graduate studies in mission theology than Johannes Verkuyl. For to be a true disciple of Jesus Christ on my continent today is to run the risk not just of stigma and dishonor, but of torture and death. A few months ago, forty-nine Jesuit priests not too far from the country I live in, were put under the threat of death by a right-wing, paramilitary organization, simply because they came to the conclusion that being a faithful disciple of Jesus in that hour implied standing alongside the millions of landless, exploited and oppressed peasants.

At the same time, a friend of mine, pastor of a large Baptist church in the capital city, was being harrassed by government officers for related reasons. He had denounced a massacre where hundreds of workers and peasants were either wounded or killed. Moreover, he had refused to condone, as other Protestant leaders appear to have done, the systematic persecution of high officials of the Catholic Church on account of their stance against human rights' violations. Finally, he had refused to accept a government offer for financial aid for the ministry of his church (the same money that had been previously allocated for the Catholic Church!), since it was not only contrary to the Baptist principle of separation of church and state, but would inhibit him from fulfilling his responsibilities as a disciple of Jesus Christ in that hour. He thus chose to keep himself free in order to denounce injustice, demand mercy, advocate a just and true peace and proclaim the fear of the Lord.[10] This stance almost cost him his life.

PARTICIPATING
IN THE MISSION OF JESUS

The call to follow has a fundamental objective: participation in the mission of Jesus. This mission is described through the imagery of fishing.

Jesus was not the first to use such a metaphor. The Old Testament sees Yahweh as a fisherman. Thus, for example, Yahweh tells Egypt: "I will put hooks in your jaws, and make the fish of your streams stick to your scales" (Ezek. 29:4). He swears that he will do the same thing with Gog" (Ezek. 38:4). Yahweh makes people "like the fish of the sea, like crawling things that have no ruler. He brings all of them up with a hook, he drags them out with his net, he gathers them in his seine" (Hab. 1:14–15). These and other Old Testament passages use the imagery of fishing to describe God's judgment on the nations. They portray God as the mighty judge, from whose "hooks" no fish, even big ones like Egypt and God, can escape.

Biblical scholars tell us that the Essene community at Qumran, which existed during the lifetime of Jesus and produced the now famous Dead Sea scrolls, kept alive the fishing metaphor from the Old Testament prophetic tradition. But whereas in the prophets God was seen as the Fisher who judges the fish of the sea, in Qumran this task was delegated to the Legitimate Teacher, otherwise identified with the promised Messiah. For its part, the noncanonical Coptic Gospel of Thomas, seems to apply the meta-phor to Jesus as the Fisher par excellence.[12]

We need to go beyond the traditional interpretation of Jesus' fishing metaphor. Far from being a simple play on words, appro-priate to the situation of the four apostles, Jesus' promise was an affirmation of profound theological significance. He inverted the traditional understanding of this imagery. Rather than identify-ing it with God's judgment, he related it to God's saving grace. The waters of the Nile had been, as it were, already infested by God's impinging judgment upon the present age. In his great mercy, however, he was providing opportunity to every "fish" to be rescued from those waters. Jesus had come for this purpose and he was calling the disciples to follow him that he might turn them into "fishers of men." We are reminded of the words of the Fourth Gospel: "For God sent the Son into the world, not to condemn the world, but that the world might be saved through him. He who believes in him is not condemned; he who does not believe is condemned already" (Jn. 3:17–18a). We are also reminded of Jesus' priestly prayer recorded in the same Gospel:

> Father, the hour has come; glorify thy Son that the Son may glorify thee, since thou has given him power over all flesh, to give eternal life to all whom thou hast given him. And this is eternal life, that they know thee the only true God, and Jesus Christ whom thou has sent . . . As thou didst send me into the world, so I have sent them into the world. (Jn. 17:1b–3, 18)

To be incorporated into the new community is then not just to be led to follow Jesus, but also to be enabled to become a channel of his grace. The promise to transform Simon, Andrew, John and James into "fishermen" made implicit the continuation of Jesus' mission through the apostles, and through those who would become disciples after them. We can now see the impor-tance of keeping close to him. For as Jesus had been sent to be the channel by which God's saving grace was to be made availa-ble to the whole of humankind, so the disciples were themselves to become the channels through which God's message of grace would reach the ends of the earth.

Nowhere does it say that they were to become *by themselves* instruments of God in the salvation of women and men. It was Jesus who would enable them to become fishers. Some would feel incompetent. Others would get "cold feet" when the going got rough. Others would feel discouraged and would be tempted to give up in defeat and go back to their old trade. Jesus, however, would make it possible for them to continue.

What an extraordinary reminder for the church in traditional Christian lands during this last quarter of the Twentieth century! A church assailed and tossed about by a defeatist inferiority complex. A church filled with guilt feelings about its past shortcomings, discouraged by the seeming impotence of its present ministry, physically and psychologically tired, traumatized by the prospects of a substantial decrease in its future role in society and in the lives of its members. To this stagnant church, which appears to be retreating from the frontiers of history and entering into a new "religious isolationism,"[13] Jesus says, "Follow me and I will make you become fishers of men."

The way out of the present crisis in the North Atlantic church does not lie in the church itself: in more relevant programs, up-to-date methods and techniques, the efficiency and talent of its leadership or in a return to old patterns. Rather the way out of the present situation lies in a renewed insertion into the mission of Jesus Christ. It lies in the disposition of the church to humble itself before him, in its willingness to let him take control of its life and ministry, to let him set its missional agenda and transform its members, by his Spirit, into effective vessels of his grace.

OBEYING JESUS IN ALL THINGS

To enable believers to be inserted effectively into the mission of our Lord, we need to teach them to obey Jesus in all things. The disciples must have learned rather quickly, at least in principle, the imperative of obedience as a prerequisite for following and participating. We are told that they left what they were doing and followed him.

In Luke's version of this pericope,[14] Jesus is shown asking the disciples to push their boats into the water. Then, from a boat, he teaches the crowds who have come to hear him. Once he finishes speaking, he tells Simon to go farther out into the water and cast their nets. Simon answers that they had been out all night and had caught nothing. Still, at his word they would give it another try. And when they did, the catch was so great that they had to ask for help.

For Luke, the call to "catch men" was extended in a dynamic context. Jesus' teaching ministry and mighty deeds not only demanded obedience, but evoked it. The call to discipleship was preceded by a practical understanding of what it meant to follow Jesus. Likewise, its response was confirmed in the concrete decision to leave everything and "follow him" (Lk. 5:11). Obedience is, consequently, the prelude, the basis, and the test of true discipleship.

John Stott has stated that "The very word 'obedience' arouses hostility today. It smacks of a grovelling servility, a mindless conformity to inflexible laws, even a bondage which is destructive of the freedom and growth of responsible human beings."[15] In Scripture, however, obedience is neither blind acceptance of inflexible laws nor conformity to rigid ideology. To obey, in the biblical tradition, means to incline one's ear, to listen in faith and to respond by faith to God's Word. That process is overshadowed, on the one hand, by the natural human disinclination to hear and believe God's Word, and, on the other, by Jesus' own perfect obedience. It is by faith in him that women and men can enter into dialogue with God's Word.

Now, when by faith in Christ we incline our ears to his Word, we discover that it does not impose upon us useless burdens, like those the scribes used to impose upon the Jews of their day. Christ's "yoke is easy" and his "burden is light" (Mt. 11:30). When we submit ourselves by faith to his Word we realize that it is not only able to "instruct [us] for salvation," but is also "profitable . . . for training in righteousness" (2 Tim. 3:15–16). Then we find ourselves saying with the psalmist: "Oh, how I love" your Word; it is "a lamp to my feet and a light to my path"; its "sum . . . is truth"; it makes the simple wise and enlightens the eyes.

Obedience in all things to Jesus' teachings is the ultimate goal, but his teachings are neither static nor totally detailed for us in Scripture. To be sure, insofar as Jesus is the fulfillment of all God's promises and has been made Lord of all, the whole of Scripture constitutes the sum total of his teachings. Throughout its pages there are specific commandments that we are called to

observe. Yet not all the teachings of Scripture are specific commandments, and even those portions that *are* may need to be
contextualized in different types of situations. A lot of the teachings found in the Bible come to us as axioms. They too need to
be contextualized in our respective cultures in order to serve
effectively as moral guides. How then can we determine what is
the will of Christ for our life-situations?

We must remember that the aim of the gospel is to set us free
from the bondage of sin and death and to restore us to our full
humanity in Jesus Christ. This puts us in the perspective of love,
since the new humanity that God has offered in Jesus Christ is
characterized by the capacity to love and to be loved. In this
respect, the fundamental function of Scripture is to enable us to
"comprehend . . . what is the breadth and length and height and
depth . . . [of] the love of Christ" (Eph. 3:18–19). The first principle
for determining the will of Christ for our respective situations is,
therefore, the principle of love: How do our particular contexts
enable us better to understand the love of Christ? And what are
the most effective ways of expressing that love?

We must also remember that interpretation of Christ's teachings is the province of the Spirit. *He,* said Jesus, "will teach you
all things, and bring to your remembrance all that I have said to
you" (Jn. 14:26). These are not separate functions but part of the
same process. To teach is to communicate and to communicate
one must make constant reference to memory. Elsewhere in the
Gospel of John, Jesus refers to the Spirit as the one who will bear
witness to him, guiding his disciples "into all the truth" and
speaking to them the words of Jesus. Whatever else can be said
about the Spirit's function in the transmission of the Word, this
much is certain: he is the dynamic force behind the translation
of the truth of Christ into our concrete life-situations. He is not
an impersonal force, not a ghost who does his thing in the world
of the invisible. Rather, he works and acts in the realm of the
historical, revealing himself, by and large, through persons and
institutions. We see signs of his presence in deeds of righteousness and love (1 Jn. 3:7, 10). To understand Christ's will, we need
to be sensitive to the work of the Spirit as the agent of righteousness and love who calls us to incarnate the truth of the gospel in
our personal and social relationships.

This means, finally, that in order to translate the teachings of our Lord adequately into our respective life-situations, we have to become thoroughly familiar with them. To be so, we shall need to experience a critical insertion into our reality. We shall need to be personally informed and involved in the basic issues of society. We shall need to be aware of the facts behind the global and particular problems of our day, and the impact they are having on the lives of our neighbors. In all of this, we shall have to have the eyes of faith wide open, reflecting on the theological significance of these facts in the light of Scripture.

To teach obedience to Jesus Christ in all things is the great challenge of world evangelization today. Everywhere we go, we are confronted with the question of what kind of disciples we are making if there is no noticeable change in their mental structure and lifestyle; if their energies are interiorized and exhausted in intrachurch activities rather than in the transformation of their history; if they make no effort to relate faith to reality; if they leave Christ out of important areas of life—like economics and politics—and reduce him to the realm of the private self or the religious club. We need to call into question discipleship programs that shun the imperative of obedience and put their emphasis on shallow slogans, that major on abstract truths and minor on concrete actions, that stress commitment to Christ without demanding the fruits of repentance, that underscore "baptism without church discipine," that permit "communion without confession" and restitution.[16]

Disciple-making is an indispensable criterion for evaluating missional faithfulness. One way to evaluate our missional program is to ask three questions: (1) Is it leading women and men to follow Jesus at each crossroad of life? (2) Is it enabling them to participate in Jesus' mission in the world? (3) Is it teaching them to obey him in all things?

Following, participating and obeying. These are marks of authentic discipleship and of a faithful Christian mission.

CHAPTER III

MISSION AS MOBILIZATION

Of all the tasks attributed to the pastoral ministry, none is so comprehensive and crucial as mobilizing the faithful for witness. This is true for at least two reasons.

From a theological perspective, believers need to be mobilized because they have been entrusted with the responsibility of penetrating every aspect of life with the gospel. The New Testament refers to this responsibility as a commission. Jesus Christ has commissioned all believers to share the good news with others. The propagation of the gospel is thus not an optional "take it or leave it" affair. It is not a matter of whether Christians like it or not or whether they feel they should do it because the pendulum has once more swung in that direction. On the contrary, the responsibility of believers to bear witness to Jesus Christ is a categorical imperative. Their evangelistic mobilization is a theological necessity, *i.e.*, it is foundational to their confession of faith in Jesus Christ as Lord of their lives.

The mobilization of believers is also a practical necessity. "The expansion of any movement is in direct proportion to its success in mobilizing its total membership in continuous propagation of its beliefs," said R. Kenneth Strachan.[1] In other words, the growth of the church depends on the effective mobilization of its members.

After the Holy Spirit, the key to this endeavor is the pastoral leadership. More than anyone else, pastors through their ministry of preaching and teaching have access to the minds and hearts of their congregation.

DEFINING MOBILIZATION

What is involved in mobilizing believers for witness? To mobilize is, first of all, to motivate: to induce people to do something; to set them in motion; to spark the fire necessary to lead them to take some kind of action. In evangelism, to motivate a congregation is to get it going in the direction of its witnessing vocation, to get it to share its faith with others.

To mobilize is, second, to recruit—in this case, to recruit believers and their resources, personal and collective, for witness. This involves making them aware of the importance and nature of witness-bearing. Although every believer is called upon to be a witness, not all believers can or should witness in the same way. Everyone is given different gifts and is placed in different situations. Just as all team members do not participate in a game in the same way, so in evangelism all believers do not play the same role. All, however, can and must be prepared to explain personally the meaning of the faith when circumstances are propitious.

Third, evangelistic mobilization requires organization. Believers must be active in whatever aspects of the church's witnessing task to which God has called them. This calls for a coordinated effort into which each can fit and have a part. Without such coordination, the mobilization of believers is truncated and becomes a frustrating experience. It is like a team that spends all its time training and receiving pep talks from the coach, without ever playing a real game.

Finally, to mobilize is to supervise. Supervision means to be on the lookout for trouble areas in the practical outworking of the evangelistic effort. It means to be ready to adjust and adapt programs to new situations. It means spending time with believers, particularly, helping them do their task effectively. Supervision means to be consistent in implementing the program, but doing it with imagination, always looking for new ways to help God's people fulfill their calling.

UNDERSTANDING
THE PROCESS OF MOBILIZATION

The foregoing premises point to a dynamic process. To understand it, we need to see how it works. How, then, does the mobilization process appear in the Christian community?

CONSCIENTIZATION   The mobilization process starts with awakening the evangelistic conscience of the people of God. To be mobilized, God's people must be made aware of their missional calling. They must be made aware of their personal responsibility as members of a community called from darkness to light and, directed by God to bear witness to his love in Jesus Christ.[2] Negatively, this means helping them to get rid of the false notion that God's mission is somehow to be carried out by religious professionals. Positively, it means enabling the people of God to accept their evangelistic charge.

The mobilization process implies, then, the declericalization of evangelism, the transference of the apostolate to the whole church. That requires, on the one hand, a self-conscientization on the part of the clergy—i.e., self-awareness and acceptance of the fact that they are neither stars nor impresarios but servants of God in the edification of his people for ministry. The congregation, on the other hand, need to see themselves not as "gap fillers" but as the true agents of God's mission who have, in their pastors, certain resources for fulfilling their joint apostolate in the world.

Awakening the church's evangelistic conscience implies also enabling it to come to grips with the gospel's deeper dimensions and with the comprehensiveness of the evangelistic vocation. It is not enough for believers to take their calling seriously. They have to understand what is the message they are to share and the multitudinous ways by which they may do so. They will thus be prepared to share in words and deeds, personally and corporately, what God has done for and in them and what is the meaning of the lordship and saving work of Christ in the light of the conflicts and struggles of women and men everywhere.

ANALYSIS   A second stage in the mobilization process is to discover the concrete reality in which believers find themselves. This involves an analysis of the congregation and the society of which it is part.

In relation to the congregation, there needs to be a diagnosis of its life in mission. This means a gathering of concrete facts about itself: rate and pattern of numerical growth; nature and type of leadership; content and style of worship; financial resources and forms of distribution; composition of support and action groups; corporate participation and personal involvement of members in the struggles and problems of society; and types of educational and missionary action programs.

Churches tend to grow lopsidedly. They tend to move like a pendulum—at times they put their emphasis on a given aspect of their ministry, at other times they tackle something else. Often they do this unconsciously. At times they think they are doing what they should—until they are objectively confronted with their behavior. A congregational analysis permits parishioners to take a hard look at "where they are at."

A congregational analysis is incomplete, however, without a parallel diagnosis of the sociohistorical reality in which the congregation lives and ministers. This implies at least a minimal understanding of its historical development: the economic, political, social, cultural and religious factors and processes that have shaped it. Since no society exists in a vacuum, or comes into being out of nowhere, to appreciate its history one has to discover its connection with global history. Then, one has to have at least a minimal vision of how that connection has affected the origen and growth of the church in general and the congregation in particular in that society.

Beyond a historical perspective, one would need at least a minimal understanding of the institutions that are actually shaping the destiny of one's society: what they are, how they are structured, in what ways they affect everyday life and where they stand in relation to the demands of the Christian faith.

These considerations point to the need for intelligent observation. At the congregational level, there must be careful observation of the effectiveness of people, talents and methods. Such observation will avoid a common error: putting people to work in the wrong place. At the societal level, there must be careful identification of the values of the surrounding community, their style of life and their major interests (personal and collective). This will permit the building of bridges for more effective communication.

PLANNING Effective mobilization involves planning for action on the basis of what has been observed and analyzed. Too often we learn a lot about people—their needs, characteristics, etc.—but fail to relate it to our aims. In evangelistic mobilization, we need to bear in mind that analysis is useless unless it leads to hard, bold evangelistic planning.

Effective planning requires, among other things: (1) goal setting; (2) selection of materials, personnel and methods; and (3) tactical preparation (what comes first, second, third, simultaneously, etc.).

Goal setting is important because it permits people to think about where they ought to go and to check themselves on the way. Are they going in the right direction? If not, why not? In evangelism, Christians need to differentiate between ultimate and penultimate goals. Ultimate goals are the comprehensive objectives of God's mission to the world: creating a new humanity through faith in Jesus Christ, and by the power of his Spirit; bringing about a new order of life by his redemptive and righteous rule through the Spirit; totally transforming history and the cosmos by the Spirit's eschatological action at the second coming of Christ. Penultimate goals, however, have to do with what a body of believers feels it must do to work systematically toward the accomplishment of ultimate goals.

For example, if in the stage of analysis a congregation discovers that its rate of numerical growth is very good but that it is not growing as well in other areas of its life, in the planning stage the satisfaction of such needs would become penultimate goals. That is, growth in other areas would become program priorities (without, of course, reducing what is already being done). Suppose, on the other hand, that a given congregation has been using an evangelistic approach which in the stage of analysis is shown to be unproductive. In the planning stage, the development of more effective evangelistic methods would become a programmatic goal.

Selection of materials, personnel and methods is contingent upon the setting of program goals. The idea here is to prepare materials, to recruit specific personnel for the different tasks needing to be done, and to select methods that will best serve to accomplish the set goals. In all of this, however, the mobilizing of as many believers as possible must be kept in mind. Otherwise one can fall into the "professional rut," developing a top-notch program with few actors and many spectators. Such a development kills any mobilization effort because it limits participation to an elite. To avoid that, there needs to be the involvement of local human resources in selecting and preparing materials, distributing program responsibilities and elaborating adequate methods.

Tactical preparation is important for effective communication. Too often goals are not reached because the way to reach them has been rough and rugged. People have to be brought to do things *a step at a time.* Accordingly, in planning for evangelistic mobilization, one needs to think about possible obstacles that might hinder the process. This will not only permit the anticipation of problems, but it will make more effective communication possible.

For such planning to serve effectively in the mobilization process, it must be done in community. Participation in the planning stage is an indispensable evidence of being mobilized for witness. No outside specialist can do the planning for a group of people and expect them to be adequately mobilized. People need to do their own goal-setting if the goals are to be accomplished by them. They need to be involved in the decision-making process if they are to carry out the decisions.

COORDINATION   Effective mobilization also involves putting into action what has been planned in a coordinated effort. This requires a functional, flexible and adaptable program. If the program is too rigid, it must be loosened up. If it is too loose, it must be tightened. If it does not appeal to autochthonous cultural symbols—that is, if it does not respond to the questions people are raising, if it does not "scratch where it itches"—it must be made more relevant.

EVALUATION   To guarantee relevance, there needs to be continuous, endless evaluation. Unless a mechanism of evaluation is inserted from the beginning, the mobilization process will be headed for failure and ineffectiveness. It will suffer from inadequate supervision, goal-checking, and continuation (follow-up). That, in turn, will likely bring about frustration and setbacks in the advances of the gospel.

TAKING NOTE OF THE CONDITIONS
FOR EFFECTIVE MOBILIZATION

Three basic conditions must be met to guarantee an effective mobilization process.

MENTAL TRANSFORMATION   First, there is the need to undergo a transformation of mind. The mobilization of the church is bound to clash with several traditional concepts. The idea of a pastor-oriented church is challenged by the parishioner-oriented character of mobilization. The tendency toward program-centeredness is difficult to overcome. That is, a given program is (functionally if not theoretically) seen as an end and not as a means, or is at best geared to attracting new people—as a show attracts spectators, or as a store sale attracts new shoppers. A program-centered approach is challenged by a goal-oriented approach, where the program varies according to specific objectives and where the thrust lies in lay witness.

There is, further, a necessary reevaluation of the specific contribution of outside leaders. Whereas in traditional evangelism (campaign or crusade evangelism, for instance), a great deal of emphasis is placed on outside leadership (an evangelist, a coordinator, Christian artists, etc.), in mobilization evangelism the emphasis is on *local leadership*. Outside leaders are viewed only as *resource persons*. The local people are the center of the action.

To all of this must be added the emphasis on a centripetal-centrifugal movement on the part of the body of believers. This challenges the idea that the church is to be found only in the gathered congregation as well as the notion that the church is only to be found in the *diaspora*—those dispersed in mission through-out the world. Where there is true and effective mobilization the church plays a double role: (1) that of a community being *brought together* by the Holy Spirit and the Word for empowering, instruc-tion, analysis and planning; and (2) that of a team being *sent* into the world *to learn* how to serve the world, *to bear witness* for Christ by word and deed, *to be redemptively present* in the struggles of the world and *to call people* to enter the kingdom of God.

Some pastors are so traditional in their thinking that they find it hard to cope with the idea of a mobilized church. Many, how-ever, have opened themselves to the idea of a parishioner-ori-ented church, a goal-oriented strategy and a coming-going body. In so doing they have experienced something of what Paul had in mind: "Do not be conformed to this world but be transformed by the renewal of your mind, that you may prove what is the will of God, what is good and acceptable and perfect" (Rom. 12:2).

SACRIFICIAL ACTION   A second condition for the church's effective mobilization is being willing to make sacrifices—that is, being willing to spend time (lots of it) in preparation, in ministry, in evaluation. It also means being willing to put the necessary resources, financial and others, at the service of the integral growth of the church. Too many people say they want results but are not willing to pay the price. They say they want growth but are not willing to work to achieve it. They say they want to live meaningful lives for the kingdom but are not willing to *rearrange their priorities.* Mobilization for evangelism is not a pastime, a hobby, or a programmatic appendix to be carried out once a month, or one or two weeks of the year. It demands the *total time* of a given congregation because it presupposes that the church exists for that.

COMPREHENSIVE FAITH   No mobilization is possible with-out a comprehensive faith. Such a faith is the capacity to believe in the God who raised our Lord Jesus Christ from the dead and made him Lord over all things. That God "from of old, is work-ing salvation in the midst of the earth" (Ps. 74:12). That God has called the church to disciple "all nations, baptizing them in the name of the Father and of the Son and of the Holy Spirit, teaching them to observe" whatever he has commanded. That God has promised to be with the church to the end of the world (Mt. 28:19–21). Do we have faith in such a God?

UNDERSCORING THE ROLE OF PREACHING AND TEACHING IN MOBILIZATION

We come to the gist of our burden. What is the role of the "ministry of the Word" in the mobilization process? Or in other terms: How can the preaching and teaching ministry of the pastor stimulate, promote and enhance the mobilization of the church?

THE WORD AS A MOTIVATIONAL FORCE   We should think of the active ministry of the Word, first of all, as a motivational force in the mobilization process. Through its proclamation and teaching, the Word of God can set on fire for service women, men, young people, even children. "Is not my word like fire, says the Lord" to Jeremiah? (Jer. 23:29). The author of Hebrews assures us that the Word of God "is living and active, sharper than any two-edged sword, piercing to the division of soul and spirit, of joints and marrow, and discerning the thoughts and intentions of the heart" (Heb. 4:12).

Now "fire" and "sword" are not only symbols of judgment. They also may stand for constructive action. Fire reminds us of fuel, combustion and forward movement. A sharp sword can symbolize an instrument that reaches the inner parts of our being, stimulating our consciences and forcing us to move ahead.

The Word of God, rightly proclaimed and taught,[3] awakens the evangelistic conscience of the church. It reminds believers that evangelism is not a "take it or leave it" affair but a *must* in the life of every Christian. It is not a "franchise" nor the sole responsibility of the ordained ministry. Rather, evangelism is the responsibility of the *laos,* the whole people of God. The Word of God also provides the necessary knowledge of the good news of God, the spiritual assurance to enable every believer to become a faithful witness—interpreting the gospel in all areas of life, leading others to Christ and building them up in faith.

In order for the preaching and teaching of the Word to motivate the body of Christ for evangelism it must be accompanied by the dynamic presence of the Holy Spirit and a contagious evangelistic setting (atmosphere). There is no serious confrontation with the Word in which the Spirit is not active and does not turn the face of the community to its witnessing vocation. There is no evangelistic setting without the action of the Holy Spirit and the Word. Neither is there any action of the Spirit in which the Word is not actively present and does not create an evangelistic consciousness.

We must seek, therefore, to complement our preaching and teaching with a vibrant, contagious evangelistic atmosphere. Our hymns and prayers, the announcements we make in our services, our church school, personal visitation, support and action groups, the decorations of our church buildings, the church bulletin, even our boards and business meetings, all should breathe an evangelistic atmosphere. They should emphasize in one way or another the imperative, comprehensiveness, privilege and opportunities for evangelism today.

We must also seek to put our preaching and teaching under the Holy Spirit's guidance and power. "A sermon," said Dietrich Bonhoeffer, "is relevant only when God is there. He is the one who makes its message concrete."[4] This is so because he alone has power to cause the necessary comprehension, acceptance and internalization of his Word to enable the hearers to put it into practice. As Jean-Jacques von Allmen declares, "Without the work of the Holy Spirit, the Word which God has spoken to the world in His son cannot be effectively translated or made present."[5] This is why the preacher-teacher needs to be a person of prayer, because prayer is the means by which we express our dependence on the Holy Spirit, seek his guidance and submit to his will. Thus through submission and intense supplication we may claim the empowering presence of the Spirit in our preaching and teaching and thus we may anticipate believers being motivated for witness.

THE WORD AS RESOURCE FOR RECRUITMENT   The ministry of the Word is not only a motivational force in the mobilization process. It is also a potential recruiting resource. If people can be motivated by the Word, they can also be recruited. The ministry of the Word offers the preacher-teacher the opportunity to take his or her congregation a step beyond recognition of their responsibility in the church's evangelizing task. The ministry of the Word provides believers with the opportunity to *do something* about the challenge they receive from God's Word.

To be an effective recruiting resource, the preacher-teacher should show how believers can participate in evangelism. He or she should visualize the kinds of things the "ordinary people" of God can do to share their faith. Biblical, historical and contemporary models of Christians who have responded affirmatively to God's call to evangelism should be presented from the pulpit. God's people should be encouraged to respond right where they are. They should be assured from the pulpit that God wants to use them as they are, with their gifts and limitations. They need to know that to the extent they let themselves be used by the Holy Spirit, their lives will be enriched, their faith will be enlarged, their joy will increase, their love for people will be strengthened and their hope in the Lord will expand.

THE WORD AS INTERPRETER OF REALITY   Third, the ministry of the Word can function as an interpreter of reality. We have argued that the mobilization of the church requires an understanding of both the internal situation of the community of faith and the sociohistorical context in which evangelism takes place. If this understanding is to strengthen the church's evangelizing endeavor, it is crucial that the results of that analysis be shared with the congregation. Many studies are being conducted these days about the inner and outer reality of the church, the findings of which never get beyond a selected number of church leaders. The consequence is that, for all their value, such studies never fulfill their educational potential. The information gathered never gets funneled to the people that matter, the persons in the pew.

It is not simply a matter of sharing with the congregation the bare facts about its life and ministry and the context of its apostolate. What is needed in the mobilization process is a biblical and theological interpretation of those facts. Churches need not only to find out where they and their surrounding world are at present. They need to be made aware of the meaning of their situation. This is a fundamental dimension of preaching and teaching.

A friend and former student of mine recently took up the pastorate of a large but troubled Presbyterian church in Puerto Rico. The first thing he did was to undertake an analysis of the congregation's social context. He then began to structure his preaching and teaching ministry along the lines of his findings, interpreting the "life in mission" of his congregation and its context in biblical and theological terms. He said to me, "I now have preaching and teaching material for the next two years!" His research has given direction to his preaching and teaching. It has also provided a platform for unveiling the internal and external reality of his congregation, a task that is basic to the mobilization process.

THE WORD AS A PROGRAM PROMOTER   My friend's experiment takes us a step further in the mobilizing function of preaching and teaching. He has not only structured his message so as to address the issues discovered in his research, but he has taken the facts to his board of elders and together with them has restructured the church's outreach. Thus his preaching and teaching ministry not only interprets the church's inner and outer reality, and motivates and recruits the membership for evangelism, but it also promotes various aspects of its *new* evangelistic program.

The ministry of the Word can be an effective promoter of a mobilization program. It can undergird its various aspects with biblical and theological material. It can persuade and encourage church members to participate and support the program. Above all, it can create an atmosphere of enthusiasm and expectant hope.

In the last several decades the Christian church in the West seems to have succumbed to an inferiority, minority and defeatist complex. It is time to snap out of it. This can be done only through a vigorous mobilization of its constituency for a continuous, in-depth propagation of the gospel. Thus the church will speak to the fears, conflicts and struggles of women and men in city streets, lonely villages, and far-out farms and jungles.

CHAPTER IV

MISSION
AS INTEGRAL GROWTH

"The Church exists by mission, just as fire exists by burning," said the late Emil Brunner.[1] In the Bible the image of fire is associated with the dynamic action of the Holy Spirit. Thus John the Baptist said to his disciples, "I baptize you with water . . . but he who is coming after me . . . will baptize you with the Holy Spirit and with fire" (Mt. 3:11). On the day of Pentecost there appeared to the disciples "tongues as of fire" (Acts 2:3).

In the New Testament, the Holy Spirit's action is always oriented toward growth. This is clear in the book of Acts where the Spirit is presented in an expanding activity, from the upper room to Samaria, to Joppa, to Antioch, to Macedonia and Rome. The church, born and kept alive by the Holy Spirit, is caught up in his ongoing activity. Accordingly, a fundamental sign of the true church is its participation in the Spirit's expanding action.

God wants and expects his church to grow—but not lopsidedly, not abnormally. He wants his church to grow in *breadth*, numerically, as an apostolic community. He wants his church to grow in *depth*, experientially, organically and conceptually, as a worshiping and nurturing community. He wants his church to grow in *height*, as a visible model, a sign of the new order of life introduced by Jesus Christ which is challenging this world's powers and principalities. In this chapter, I want to zero in on these three aspects of church growth.

GROWING IN BREADTH

First, the question of numerical growth. This is particularly related to the church's apostolic character. The word *apostle* is linked to the idea of mission, mobility and extension. An apostle in the New Testament was one sent to make disciples. The church is an apostolic community because it is the heir of the apostles' message and commission.

For a long time western christendom, forgetting this mark of the church, emphasized its unity, sanctity and catholicity: one holy catholic church. It was not until recently that it began to repossess the church's apostolicity (*i.e.*, its sent-out, missionary character) as a fundamental dimension of its nature.

As an apostolic community, the church is to participate in a continuous process of expansion so that it may spread the gospel and actualize its power in the world. The church is not merely sent *to* but *in*to all the world. We see this illustrated in two of our Lord's parables.

> He said therefore, "What is the kingdom of God like? And to what shall I compare it? It is like a grain of mustard seed which a man took and sowed in his garden; and it grew and became a tree, and the birds of the air made nests in its branches." And again he said, "To what shall I compare the kingdom of God? It is like leaven which a woman took and hid in three measures of flour, till it was all leavened." (Lk. 13:18–21)

The church is a sign of God's kingdom. It is the kingdom's most concrete, historical manifestation. Hence, it can be called the community which emodies the kingdom's life and purpose. As such, the church is to be on the march, spreading the seed of the gospel in God's garden (the world) so that the seed may become a tree with ever-growing branches. In this process, the church is also to leaven every sector of humankind with the power of the gospel. The church is to grow in order to communicate the good news and bring about, in the power of the Holy

Spirit, new communities that leaven the world. There are those who want to see the church participate in the transformation of the world without reproducing itself into lively and committed communities. Others want to see it reproduce itself without fermenting their own environment with the kingdom's transforming power.

Jesus and the early Christian church refused to accept such a split. For them, the guarantee of the gospel's fermenting action was the lively, committed communities of believers, spreading into ever-growing branches. The test of authenticity of these growing communities was their leavening action in the world.

The crucial question for most Christians is not whether growth in breadth is important. Most Christians pay lip service, in one way or another, to the need to expand numerically. The key question for most of them is this: How can the church grow? How can it reproduce itself into communities that will be active in the world? Or to put it in other terms: How can the church move from the *ought* to the *is*, from acceptance of the need to expand numerically to a real experience of growth?

SOWING   I live in a small agrarian country. Costa Rica lives off the fruit of the ground. Some have called it a dessert-producing country because its chief products heretofore have been bananas and coffee. Be that as it may, the fact is that Costa Ricans thrive on agriculture, and I have had to learn to look at the Bible with agricultural eyes. I have been helped by people like C. Peter Wagner, who in his book *Frontiers in Mission Strategy* has pointed out several agricultural principles related to church growth.[2] Following Wagner's suggestions and the intuitions gathered from my own context, let me underscore several principles that help us deal with the above question.

There is, first, the principle of sowing. A farmer, says the Gospel story,

> went out to sow. And as he sowed, some seeds fell along the path, and the birds came and devoured them. Others fell on rocky ground, where they had not much soil, and immediately they sprang up, since they had no depth of soil, but when the sun rose they were scorched; and since they had no root they withered away. Other seeds fell upon thorns, and the thorns grew up and choked

them. Other seeds fell on good soil and brought forth grain, some a hundredfold, some sixty, some thirty. He who has ears, let him hear. (Mt. 13:3–9)

This parable confronts us with the different types of soil where the seed of the gospel may fall. Understood in its context, it also shows us various responses to the gospel. By implication, however, the parable reminds us that not all those who are evangelized respond in the same manner, and of those that hear, only a few make a lasting response. It also reminds us of the responsibility of the farmer, which in this case would be the Christian or the church. The responsible church will sow intelligently, not haphazardly. The church's task is not merely to spread the Word, but to do so intelligently. This means that it needs to test the soil. The problem with many Christians and with a lot of churches is that they tend to be like a farmer who has a blindfold over his or her eyes and lets the seed fall wherever it falls, not worrying whether it lands on rocky ground, along the path, or among thorns. The church and its members need to think intelligently, if for no other reason than that God has given them multiple gifts to enable them to identify the different types of soil.

To sow intelligently also means that we need to discern where God is at work and sow accordingly. In agriculture, there is something the farmer does, but there is also something nature does. My job takes me all over Latin America. Everywhere I go, I have been able to witness what natural catastrophies do to agriculture; they can destroy the entire crop of a nation or region. A lot of the success of harvest depends not just on the farmer's faithfulness, but on that *plus* factor that is given by nature. In world evangelization, that *plus* factor is God. Not only must we test the soil to see whether it offers good farming possibilities, but we must discern where God is at work. We must do it by being sensitive to the Spirit and the Word, which lead us and guide us to areas that have the better possibilities of harvest. We must do this intelligently, observing the responses being given to the Word in specific situations. This is why I believe in the value of the social sciences for evangelism. They help us undertake studies that give the information we need.

In evangelistic ministry we often make mistakes because we do not take hold of resources that have come our way. We tend to get uptight about the integrity of our message, while forgetting the scientific resources that God has given us to make the message more effective. Behind that attitude, of course, there is a poor theology.

CULTIVATION Cultivation is a second principle. Not only must the soil be tested, it must be well taken care of. We recall Paul's words: "I planted, Apollos watered, but God gave the growth" (1 Cor. 3:6). In the context of Corinth, this principle was applied to the church's inner life. Planting and watering of God's people was necessary for God to give growth. It still is. We have to motivate the people of God. We have to create an appropriate atmosphere in the church. We have to prepare God's people for evangelism. Pastors and church leaders often expect their people to go out and share their faith with others. But when those individuals come to church, they do not find a vibrant evangelistic atmosphere. If there is no prayer for the salvation of people, if there is no singing about the challenge of and opportunities for evangelism, if pastors do not talk up the good news with their parishioners, if in their house calls and counseling sessions pastors do not encourage believers to think about those who are outside the frontiers of the faith, then how can they expect the laity to be motivated to evangelize their friends and neighbors? The evangelistic cultivation of the church is necessary for growth to take place. Growth may be from God, but we have to do our share. God will never do for us what we are supposed to do for ourselves.

The same can be said about the church's outreach ministry. We can keep ourselves so busy sowing that we fail to cultivate the ground adequately. And so we saturate the ground with seed, we bombard it with John 3:16 and the likes, only to find the ground so hard that there is no way it can be productive.

In Cuenca, Ecuador, there was in 1970 an outwardly successful evangelistic campaign, part of the Evangelism In Depth (E/D) movement in that country. Something unusual occurred there. Cuenca is Ecuador's third largest city, with a population (at the time of the campaign) of 125,000. It has often been called "the Athens of Ecuador" because of its university and old traditions. It is culturally and religiously a conservative city.

At the time of E/D there were three small Protestant congregations with a total membership of no more than 75. One of these churches was Lutheran. A few years after it started working in Cuenca, the Lutheran mission decided to open a day school which drew a lot of children but was not able to convince them and their parents to come to church.

Then came evangelist Paul Finkenbinder to hold a campaign from June 23–28, 1970. A downtown theater was rented, a choir was rehearsed, ushers and counselors were trained. Finkenbinder had been known in Cuenca through his radio program, "A Message to the Conscience," and was popularly known as *Hermano Pablo* (Brother Paul). According to Paul Pretiz,

> the influence of the mass media (HCJB [a powerful Protestant radio station that transmits out of Quito and has evangelistic] programs on commercial stations via its Guayaquil center [and] 'Hermano Pablo's' radio program), the Lutheran [Day] School, and the liberalizing influence of the university and world events (Vatican Council, etc.) prepared the way for a positive response to the Gospel.[3]

The name of Hermano Pablo seemed to have created immense curiosity among the inhabitants of Cuenca; evening meetings averaged around 1,300. That response was aided by the fact that "for four nights Hermano Pablo had a TV audience-talk show. The services themselves were also broadcast." No one is certain how many people responded to the invitation to receive Jesus Christ as Lord and Savior; responses were en masse. "It was impossible to counsel with each inquirer," says Pretiz. One source "states the number was about 1,224; another source gives 1,130; the [official report of the Evangelism In Depth assembly] mentions 669 decisions on cards."

Two years later Pretiz went to Cuenca in order to see what was left of the "fruits" of the campaign. His report[4] was not very flattering. He states:

> Considering the people who attribute their conversion to Evangelism in Depth and who are now in evangelical churches, we may estimate that 30 of the present members may be traceable to the movement. No doubt others were influenced, as was the case with some who stated they attended the campaign before accepting Christ. Church membership before and after the campaign may be compared in the following summary:

CHURCH	BEFORE E/D, 1969	AFTER E/D, 1972
Lutheran	44 *(one church)*	80 *(two churches)*
Independent	15	18
Assemblies of God	15 *(estimate)*	20 *(estimate)*
Baptist	—	11
Interamerican	—	13
Totals	74	142

Those results are not impressive if we consider the tremendous turnout for the campaign and the reported number of inquiries made during the meetings. It is in order, therefore, for us to ask what happened. Pretiz has made several suggestions, two of which seem to me the most relevant. First, he notes that the people who responded to the gospel in the Cuenca meeting represented a particular type of inquirer, namely, "the person who is perhaps somewhat disenchanted with Roman Catholicism, who can manifest his agreement with the statements of the Gospel as made in the campaign, but who finds his social frames of reference still so strong that he cannot conceive of leaving the Roman Church." In other words, the sociocultural milieu of the people did not allow them to follow through with their decision and join a Protestant church. Second, he points out that

> there was such a loss in the transfer of the public's acceptance of "Hermano Pablo" to an acceptance of the [Protestant] church that many local lay pastors seemed unprepared and uninspiring by comparison with the charisma that surrounded the evangelist. The implication is that any long-term effort may demand upgrading the style and content of the local pastor's ministry in both its spiritual and intellectual dimension as part of an evangelistic movement.[5]

The result of Pretiz's study left many Christian leaders somewhat confounded. Four and a half years later, I visited the Bishop of the Episcopal Church of Ecuador. He shared with me a document (of the *Iglesia Episcopal de Ecuador*) describing the outstanding numerical growth experienced by his church since 1971, when it had 161 members in the entire country.[6] By 1976, this church had 2,015 members, with 21 organized missions, 37 mission stations and 2 English-speaking chaplaincies. As I browsed through the

report, I discovered that one area where the church had experienced growth, emerging as it were out of nowhere in the last
two years, was in the city of Cuenca. There in 1976 it had two
missions and two mission stations with a total communicant
membership of 100. I asked him about this and he commented
that they had entered Cuenca at the invitation of some Roman
Catholics who were not satisfied with the spiritual nourishment
they were getting in their own church. The Bishop decided to
send a well-equipped clergy to Cuenca. The result was a positive
permanent response in a city that has represented a tough ground
for Protestant churches and in a church that is not supposed to
grow numerically in Latin lands!

In the one case the soil had been cultivated, but not the inner
life of the church. In the other there was a lot of care to accompany the fertile soil, with special pastoral leadership to follow up
the kind of interest shown in the gospel. I have a hunch, though
I cannot verify it, that it was not until there was adequate care
for the inner life of the church, through top-quality leadership,
that the openness shown to the gospel in 1970 began to show
permanent results.

PRUNING   We must not only sow and cultivate the soil. We
must also prune dead branches. We have to be careful that we do
not fall into the syndrome of endless cultivation. The parable of
the fig tree is a good reminder.

> A man had a fig tree planted in his vineyard; and he came seeking
> fruit on it and found none. And he said to the vine dresser, "Lo,
> these three years I have come seeking fruit on this fig tree, and I
> find none. Cut it down; why should it use up the ground?" And he
> answered him, "Let it alone, sir, this year also, till I dig about it and
> put on manure. And if it bears fruit next year, well and good; but
> if not, you can cut it down." (Lk. 13:6–9)

We have to apply the principle of trial and error if we are to
grow in breadth. On a first level, this means that we ought to be
ready to move into a new section of town, a new city, or a new
group of society, wherever our sowing and cultivation do not
produce adequate results. I am not advocating the unqualified
abandonment of a field just because there is no fruit. We must
learn to wait upon the Lord.

I'll never forget the day, two years ago, when at a consultation on church growth a missionary from the Middle East sadly said to me: "You know, I've been in the Middle East thirty years and I have never had the privilege of leading one single Muslim to Jesus Christ." What does one say to such a person? Thirty years! I said: "Well, compare your thirty years with the more than one thousand years in which Christians have acted so uncharitably and so unmission-like with the Muslim world. Our failure in the past forces us now to be patient, to re-prepare the soil, to endure in the work and wait upon the Lord. You just have to hang in there."

The late Max Warren, in his book *I Believe in the Great Commission,* tells of one of the nineteenth-century pioneers in Iran who said of his missionary work: "I am not reaping the harvest; I scarcely claim to be sowing the seed; I am hardly plowing the soil; but I am gathering out the stones. That too is missionary work; let it be supported by loving sympathy and fervent prayer."[7]

It is one thing to be faithful, remembering that we are not the stars in world evangelization. It is another thing to be poor stewards. What I'm talking about is not abandonment of the field altogether, but putting our resources into those areas where the Lord is acting—while leaving our unproductive work with a minimum, though solid witness. One day the Muslim world could turn into a harvest.

At a second level, the principle of trial and error means that we are not to fall so much in love with a given method that we cannot change it if it is no longer adequate for the desired end. I come from a group of churches in Puerto Rico that many years ago discovered an evangelistic method and somehow seemed to have forgotten that other methods exist. It almost seems that if they cannot have an evangelistic crusade, they cannot evangelize. The "campaign method" has placed them in a situation of evangelistic inflexibility. Because of this, these churches often do not grow as they should. I believe that evangelistic campaigns may have a positive impact on certain occasions, but the principle of trial and error would lead me to be critical of any situation that depended solely on it. No method is a sacred cow. Therefore if we are going to be faithful, we're going to have to learn by trial

and error to move on when a given method does not lead us to
the goals that we think we should be achieving.

At a third level, this principle of trial and error means that we
ought to be on the lookout for extrachurch means of spreading
the gospel. Many pastors and church leaders give the impression
of depending solely on the work of the institutional church for
the growth of the body of Christ, as if the Holy Spirit were bound
sociologically to the church and whatever it was able to accomplish. We know, however, that the Holy Spirit not only uses
political, social, economic, religious, cultural and intellectual
movements to prepare the ground for the proclamation of the
gospel, but he often works (in the last two centuries, remarkably
so) through parachurch groups. Movements and organizations
like the YMCA, church schools, Gideons, SCM, IVF and independent missionary societies continue to be extraordinary channels for the communication of the gospel around the world. We
need, therefore, to be sensitive to and grateful for mission in-
strumentalities that lie outside our institutional controls but con-
tribute to the spread of the gospel. Often they prune the work of
established ecclesiastical bodies by sowing and plowing in areas
not touched by the others' evangelistic outreach.

HARVESTING   Finally, there is the principle of the harvest.
In Evangelism in Depth we coined a slogan: "Abundant reaping requires abundant sowing." In Cuenca, Ecuador, we discovered that not only does abundant reaping require abundant
sowing, but that it also requires abundant *cultivation*. We have
also come to realize that abundant *sowing* requires abundant
cultivation, and likewise, abundant cultivation demands abundant *reaping*.

Harvest time is a critical period. You run the chance of losing
precious fruit. It requires total dedication, a total effort to reap.

In Costa Rica's rural communities, when coffee season comes,
schools are closed. Children go out into the countryside to pick
coffee beans. Everybody is caught up in the process of harvest,
because if you don't pick the fruit, there's not going to be anything to eat.

Jesus underlines the importance of looking for ripe harvest and
harvesting it quickly. "Do you not say, 'There are yet four
months, and then comes the harvest'! I tell you, lift up your eyes,

and see how the fields are already white for harvest" (Jn. 4:35). Many church leaders are like the disciples, insensitive to harvest time. They pray, "Lord, send us an awakening," and when the awakening comes, they don't see it. The fact of the matter is that they're not really prepared to give what it takes to gather the harvest.

What does it take? First, intelligent investment of time and energy in spreading the gospel. Second, patient cultivation of those who can be mobilized for evangelism and those who are to be evangelized. Third, flexibility in space and methods. Fourth, sensitivity and sacrificial dedication to the Spirit's movement in people's lives. "[They] that go forth weeping, bearing the seed for sowing, shall come home with shouts of joy, bringing [their] sheaves with [them]" (Ps. 126:6).

GROWING IN DEPTH

The church is an organism that needs to grow internally. Paul places such development at the center of ministry.

> And his gifts were that some should be apostles, some prophets, some evangelists, some pastors and teachers, to equip the saints for the work of ministry, for building up the body of Christ, until we all attain to the unity of the faith and of the knowledge of the Son of God, to mature manhood, to the measure of the statute of the fulness of Christ; so that we may no longer be children, tossed to and fro and carried about with every wind of doctrine, by the cunning of men, by their craftiness in deceitful wiles. Rather, speaking the truth in love, we are to grow up in every way into him who is the head, into Christ, from whom the whole body, joined and knit together by every joint with which it is supplied, when each part is working properly, makes bodily growth and upbuilds itself in love. (Eph. 4:11–16)

The church should not only grow in its evangelistic outreach, proclaiming the gospel and calling women, men and children to faith and repentance, but also in *depth*, by incorporating those who respond and enabling them to mature in the faith. In the above passage, Paul outlines three levels of this aspect of church growth.

CONCEPTUAL DEPTH First, there is the conceptual level, or growth in what Paul calls the unity of faith. To grow in depth is to broaden one's understanding of the Christian faith. The English word *understand* is unique. In my own language, Spanish, we cannot play around with it as we can in English, because in the latter it is made up of two words, *under* and *stand*. To understand is to get hold of what undergirds, gives foundation and sustains. To grow in depth is to help the people of God get a foundation in the Christian faith. The Christian faith is not a set of doctrines, but trust and commitment to Jesus Christ. The gospel is a person. It is Jesus the Savior, annointed by God for our salvation.

But there is a corpus of historical and theological facts attached to this person—who he was and what he did; who he is, what he is doing in our society, in our lives and in our history, where and how; who he will be and what he will do in the end of time. To believe in Christ is to have at least a minimal awareness of these facts. To grow in Christ is to be getting an ever greater grasp of them.

For Christians, Jesus Christ is the key to understanding history. His story gives meaning to our story. Faith in him requires correlation of what he has done, is doing and will do with everything we do; of his Word with our words; of his kingdom with the kingdoms of this world; of his saving power with the ongoing struggles of history.

To broaden our understanding of the Christian faith is to begin to correlate all these facts, historical and theological, about Christ with our respective life-situations. From the beginning of my theological training, I had a tremendous suspicion of theologians like Rudolf Bultmann and his students and their existentialist school of thought. Now that I have gotten into deeper questions relating to my historical context as a Puerto Rican and a Latin American; now that I've become committed to the liberation of my country and the rest of my continent from the powers of colonialism and oppression, I have increased my suspicion of the type of theology these theologians represent. At the bottom, my problem lies with their tendency to play down Jesus of Nazareth's historicity. This represents not only a theological fuzziness, but also a hidden ideological agenda. In reducing Jesus of Nazareth to an existential "Christ of faith," they create their own individual Christ, in the image and likeness of western bourgeois Christianity, and limit him thereby to certain spaces in life. Even worse, they empty him of his historical significance, namely, his power to help his followers participate in transforming their world. Without a concrete reference to the historical Jesus, Christ loses the revolutionary thrust of his mission.

To broaden our understanding of the Christian faith is to correlate the maning of Jesus Christ, all the facts about his life and ministry, with our own sociohistorical context; to ask ourselves what his life and teachings, his incarnation, death, resurrection, ascension and promised return mean in our historical situation. That is why Paul uses the expression, "until we all attain to the unity of the faith" (Eph. 4:13). In this life we will never grasp the whole meaning of Jesus Christ. He is a mystery continuously being disclosed by the Holy Spirit. Yet this mystery is rooted in a concrete person who lived in a given era and left us with clear criteria to identify his presence in history and to verify whatever insights we receive in the course of our life in mission.

We need to work to a unifying understanding of Jesus Christ. In this search we will be guided by his history. Jesus Christ is still working and moving around in the universe. But he is not the private Lord of existentialist theology, meaningful only to me. Nor is he the great ideal of nineteenth-century liberal theology, whose only power is in setting a good moral example. Rather, his present-day activity is coherent with what he did and said. We have certain criteria to discover what Christ is doing in history. We have guidelines to know where to find him and how to relate him to life.

We know, for example, that he is not a lily-white, upper-middle-class bourgeois Jesus, detached from society's poor and disenfranchised. He was a person who identified himself with people in situations of oppression and conflict. He was a preacher of the poor, a healer of the sick and a liberator of the oppressed (Lk. 4:18). He was a friend of "tax collectors and sinners" (Lk. 7:34) who was born in a stable (Lk. 2:7) and died on a cross between two criminals (Lk. 23:33).

We need constantly to be tying up the loose ends of our relationship with him into our multiple-life situations. That is how I define theology, by the way. Theology has been conceived in western Christianity as an academic ivory-tower discipline, largely on account of its traditional relationship with medieval scholasticism. Actually, theology is not an intellectual exercise for leisure time; rather, it is committed reflection. It is not something one repeats or memorizes, but rather something one does. It is tying up the loose ends of our lives from the perspective of one's faith. That is why each generation has to think through its faith. It is also the reason why theology cannot be thought of as being equivalent to faith. Theology needs to relate faith to the context of life. We *do* theology, we don't simply act as a recording machine that quotes what the old and new giants are saying.

In 1974, I was preaching in Vietnam to some 500 pastors in the central highlands. One day I had a conversation with some missionaries who were working with one of the tribes. They commented that it was difficult to teach them theology because they just didn't have the mental capacity for it. As we were eating and talking, I started observing the cloth on the table. I was intrigued by it because it looked like cloths the Indians of Guatemala make. Its design had figures that looked like helicopters, planes, machine guns, horses. I asked my hosts, "Where did you get this cloth?" They told me that one of the members of the tribes with whom they were working, in fact, a student at the Bible Institute, had done it. It then dawned on me that this man had managed to describe his entire world in that table cloth. He couldn't interpret his history in written form, nor in the language of Protestant academic theology, but he had been able to put it together in his own manner. He had artistically tied up the loose ends of his life into that tablecloth, and that made him a far better theologian than the missionaries who were serving as his theological teachers.

If we want to help Christians grow in the unity of the faith, we have to enable them to relate at the grassroots their faith in Christ to their own experiences. A church that does not reflect critically and contextually on its faith will die. It will be "tossed to and fro and carried about with every wind of doctrine" (Eph. 4:14).

This is one of the most serious problems facing the church in North America and Western Europe. Two years ago, a denominational executive said to me: "You're not telling us something new when you challenge us to grow in depth. Why, we've been doing that in mainline Protestantism for a long time! Quality growth has been the thing in our churches. A good theological content, a well-educated ministerium!" I looked at him and said: "Really? Then, why is it that whenever I read many of your theologians I sense the pragmatic, liberal, capitalistic, pop philosophy that has made up the American way of life creeping in? Why is it that there seems to be among the overwhelming majority of them so little critical interaction with their social, economic and political context? Why do I get the feeling that theology in your part of the world becomes, at times, a drag? Why is it that the exciting things in the thinking of the faith seem to have been occurring for the last several years in the periphery, with the blacks and more recently with native Americans, Asians, Hispanics and women? Why is it that there is such a gap between the ongoing life of the church and the dynamic movements and challenges that we encounter in the Bible? Why is it that so often we hear pastors say, 'You know, when I left seminary, I came out with the idea that the Bible was a dead book'?" Doing theology seems to me to have been confused in North America and Western Europe with some kind of academic gymnastics.

I am not advocating an uncritical contextualization, because western theology has been very contextual. Just look at H. Richard Niebuhr's *The Social Sources of Denominationalism*. [8] He points out that it is precisely out of their social context that North American denominations spring forth. But to be contextually critical, to be able to turn back with the questions of the faith, that's another matter. This is one of the challenges that lies before Northern American and Western European Christians: to grow conceptually, in the unity of the faith, in a critical interaction with their societies and culture and with all the presuppositions behind them—interaction with a syncretistic value system that leaves a lot to be desired when viewed from the perspective of biblical revelation.

EXPERIENTIAL DEPTH   A second level of growth in depth is that of experience: attaining to the "unity of the faith and of the knowledge of the Son of God." In the Bible, knowledge is not a body of facts but rather a profoundly experiential and relational matter.[9] That was the critical issue with the Gnostics, who prided themselves on secret and private knowledge, wanting to keep it all to themselves. And so, time and again, in the New Testament's polemic writings against the Gnostics, there is the reminder that our knowledge of the Son of God is experiential in the widest sense of the word. Especially in the Gospel and Epistles of John, our knowledge of Christ is presented as having its locus not on our ability to give right answers but on our capacity to love others. Love for others becomes the testing point of our knowledge of God. Love is the most important sign of Christian faith. "By this," says Jesus, "all men will know that you are my disciples, if you have love for one another" (Jn. 13:35).

To love others, in fact, is the only acceptable expression of our love for Christ. Paraphrasing his words in Matthew 25, if you want to express your love to me, don't come telling me about it, but rather show it to me. Go out to the prisoners, the hungry, the naked and destitute, because I am there in their midst. Jesus seems to be drawing us back to the prophetic criticism of the Old Testament: "He has showed you, O man, what is good; and what does the Lord require of you but to do justice, and to love kindness, and to walk humbly with your God?" (Mic. 6:8). That's what the true knowledge of Christ is all about: serving others and not being served. It is doing his will, even as he came to serve and not to be served.

ORGANIC DEPTH   Third, growth in depth does not become operational until it touches the organic life of the community. By organic life I mean everything that deals with the church's everyday action: persons, groups and agencies acting and interacting with one another in and outside formal boundaries. This is what Paul calls equipping the saints in order that they may engage in the work of ministry and build the body of Christ[10] (Eph. 4:12). It is a matter of stewardship, of being faithful to a calling.

Since the church has been called to be a *koinonia*, organic growth enables it to act as a *family*. There is interrelation, fellowship and sharing. Since the church is a community of disciples, organic growth enables it to be a *school*. There is education for mission. Since the church is a body, organic growth enables it to work as a *team*. Family, school, team—three contemporary traits of an old reality. Three areas in which growth has to be evident. A community that is not growing in fellowship, that does not know how to celebrate, share and pray together; a community that does not engage in learning, that does not build up its members and lead them to obey ("incline the ear to") the Word of the Master and dialogue with him as he speaks through his Word and comes to it in the Spirit; a community that does not act as a team, each of its members functioning according to their respective gifts, playing, as it were, God's ballgame—that is not the church of Jesus Christ.

The church must reflect critically on whether or not each of its parts is working properly. The job of its leaders does not end with their theoretical equipment for ministry. Leaders must take their equipping to the arena of action. They must see to it that each member, each component of that community, is actualizing the faith in the context of his or her talents and life responsibilities and in the light of the church's total mission.

It is not enough to say that pastors have mainly a teaching function. They should be seen as agents of mobilization. This applies not just to church members, but also to congregations, to city/state/regional/national and international agencies. The task of the church's pastoral leadership is to build up the body. They should be helping the church grow in depth:

conceptually, by stimulating it to work toward the unity of the faith, by stimulating every member, every congregation and agency to do theology and become a theological community;

experientially, by helping every member deepen their relationship to the Son of God and express that relationship in their lifestyle; and

functionally, by mobilizing each of its parts so that the body can engage effectively in the gospel ministry.

GROWING IN HEIGHT

A third aspect of holistic growth is related to lifestyle. In Jesus'
Sermon on the Mount we read:

> You are the light of the world. A city set on a hill cannot be hid.
> Nor do men light a lamp and put it under a bushel, but on a stand,
> and it gives light to all in the house. Let your light so shine before
> men, that they may see your good works and give glory to your
> Father who is in heaven. (Mt. 5:14–16)

That passage confronts us with a sharp biblical imperative: the
light is so to shine in our everyday life that people can see the
greatness of God's work and glorify him. Commitment to Jesus
Christ leads to experiencing his power in us. Paul said that "for
the sake of Christ" he had suffered "the loss of all things" in order
that he might "know him and the power of his resurrection," and
might "share his sufferings, becoming like him in his death"
(Phil. 3:7–10). The Christian faith is life ever-growing in the likeness of Jesus Christ. Consequently, Christians should experience
continuous growth in their lifestyles. Several reasons found in
the passage from the Sermon on the Mount substantiate this
imperative.

CHRISTIANS AS LIGHT   First, Christians should grow in their
lifestyles *because of who they are.* Jesus said, "You are the light of
the world." The scriptural concept of light has to do with revelation and ethics.[11] Light is likened to truth; darkness to falsehood.
Light is a symbol of God's kingdom. Darkness is a symbol of the
present order of life, which passes away. God is said to be light;
in him there is no darkness. Jesus is the light that shines in the
darkness and the darkness cannot overcome him. Those who
believe in him are the children of light and are exhorted to walk
in the light. To say that Christians are the light of the world is
to affirm their identity in the world. Their lives have been designed to challenge falsehood and deceit. They are to be followers
of truth, representing truth against deceit. They are to stand for
what is good and against what is evil. They are to be decision-

makers. They are to be society's moral conscience. In a world that has lost its direction, its sense of judgment, and has become morally corrupted, Christians are called to help recover that conscience and help the world make right judgments.

The Baptist pastor I referred to in chapter II, in the last days of his eighteen-year pastorate in Central America, experienced harrassment from police and government forces—not because he took a machine gun, went out to the hills and joined the guerrillas. Rather, he was trying to live out his Christian life and fulfill his ministry faithfully in the midst of a social order filled with deceit, corruption, electoral frauds, mass slaughters, oppression, repression and exploitation of defenseless peasants and workers. It was a situation in which to dare to stand for the cause of justice was a crime. He refused to bow down to an offer of financial cooperation from political authorities. He chose instead to keep his distance while denouncing the evil he saw around him. He advocated the cause of justice. His presence became offensive to the political and military authorities. Because he refused to accept deceit, to be bought and used by those authorities, he almost lost his life.

My friend is only one among a growing minority in Latin America who are engaged in living out, in a peaceful and decisive way, the life of God's kingdom. They are letting the light of the gospel shine forth in situations of extreme hatred and persecution, especially toward those who dare condemn corruption. Yet these individuals keep refusing to accept injustice as a way of life. They are demanding a just economic and social order.

As Christians, we are designed to be light. When there is darkness around us, we must shine forth.

We need to expand our consciousness of this. We need to be on the lookout for anything that tends to dim the light of the gospel in our lives.

Christians are placed in this world to be society's conscience. Therefore we cannot under any circumstances give up on social, economic, political and cultural issues. We cannot close our eyes and ears to the issues that shape our world. We cannot be neutral. We need to grow more and more in our commitment to truth, and thus to justice, love and well-being.

CHRISTIANS AS PEOPLE FOR OTHERS   Second, we are to grow in our lives *because of what we are called to do*. Christianity is personal, but it is not an individualistic faith. A person is always related to an environment, a culture, other people. In being personal, Christianity is socially oriented. Christians are expected to live exemplary lives before others. Their lives are to be transparent, reflecting the light of the kingdom—which is a new order characterized by love. Christians are to live in love. They exist for others.

I don't know any other community in the world that is specifically designed to exist for the sake of others. My Marxist friends have a strong commitment to others, but, if I understand Marxism correctly, it is a commitment informed by the hope of getting something in return, even if it is for everyone and not just for a few. In other words, their commitment is motivated by the need of a just distribution of the earth's resources and by the conviction that in sharing the fruits of human labor one is able to live more justly and meaningfully. Christians, however, are called to die for the world, to be at the service of others without expecting anything in return. This is why we are a pilgrim community, called to travel through life with little equipment.[12] Our hope lies not in a man-made city, but in the city which is to come, "whose builder and maker is God."[13] We have been set free from obsession with self and have learned to live and hope in the grace of God. For us, humanization is not a task to be accomplished but a gift to be received and shared.[14] We can thus live for others without counting the cost or expecting rewards in return. The hope of the Christian community is not escapist. It is rather an active hope that searches for something better for those at whose service Christians have been called to be. We are to be a community of justice, because the kingdom of God is an order of equitous relations. Hence, wherever Christians live and work there should be militant advocacy for justice and righteous living. Because Christians are the community of the kingdom, they are also to work for peace, and thus struggle and suffer so that women and men may experience life without persecution, harrassment, fear and want.

Church growth is not an ultimate, but a penultimate. In the

church's life and mission, the ultimate is the hope of the final consummation of God's kingdom.[15] There are those who have rightly asked whether the church, by setting its hope on that final moment, has not retrenched from the fundamental issues of history. My answer to that question is affirmative but qualified. To be sure, the church's growth is a penultimate goal of its mission. But this growth is to be measured, not simply by the number of people entering into the church's fellowship, but especially by their participation in the bringing about of a new order, in establishing a community of love, in struggling for justice and peace as an *anticipation of the ultimate revelation of God's kingdom.*

When we think of church growth in these terms, the whole thing becomes a revolutionary, powerful adventure. The axis of discussion changes. From this perspective, that demonic polarization that has split Christians in recent years, that has consummed endless energies on useless discussion, creating futile internal struggles over whether the success of our mission should be measured quantitatively or qualitatively, whether we should be concerned with spiritual or with social issues, whether our evangelistic energies should emphasize the vertical dimension of the gospel or simply limit it to its horizontal aspects—all of this begins to be eliminated when we see church growth as a provisional goal which contributes to the effective transformation of our precarious historical situation. The focus, even in such moments as in giving an evangelistic invitation or incorporating into the community of faith those who respond, is not on the internal aspects of the Christian community. Rather the church's internal aspects are focused on ministry to the world. In this case, the church is turned "inside out."[16] Its energies are directed toward the questions of history wherein the church is called to bear witness to the love, justice and peace of God's kingdom.

Christians are called to cultivate those characteristics of the kingdom in their respective historical situation. The way the life principles of the kingdom become operational vary according to our own situation. Christians need to be flexible. They should be able to live under any system and participate prophetically in it.

Whenever I return to the USA, I sense a cynical attitude among Christians in relation to what is happening in countries like socialist Cuba. I find that disturbing. It seems to be inconceivable for friends in the USA to believe that Christians there may be living faithfully, participating in the process of socialization that Cuba has been undergoing in the last decades while maintaining a critical distance from the existing order as a consequence of their faith in Jesus Christ. I get irked when I see the same attitude toward Christian brothers and sisters in eastern European countries or toward Christians who may be left in the People's Republic of China. It would almost seem as if the only place where one has the possibility of being a Christian is in western democratic capitalistic societies.

I find myself thinking "How naive, how shortsighted, how provincial can one be!" I say this bearing in mind that I too have a well-defined political and ideological position. But I do not believe that any social or economic system is a sacred cow. All systems come under the judgment of God, including western capitalism.

Social and political systems do not come to us by way of special revelation. The Bible does not give us a blueprint for society's organization. Such systems are the fruit of human competence, and in these varying systems Christians are called to grow in their lifestyle. That is, they are called to participate in them from the perspective of kingdom principles.

While I was a pastor of a Hispanic community in Milwaukee, Wisconsin, I became involved in inner-city politics. When I moved to San José, Costa Rica, I found ways of expressing my social and political responsibility. If I were to live in a socialist society, I would also have to find ways of expressing my commitment to God's kingdom. My responsibility to expand and sharpen that commitment would be a part of my mission in whatever situation I found myself.

Christians need to understand their historical and social reality in order to evaluate their faithfulness to the gospel. In North America some Christians have accepted their system uncritically, as if it were revealed from above. They refuse even to question the values that lie underneath it from the perspective of the gospel.

Pastors and church leaders are called to help others think through and evaluate the way to "incarnate" God's new order of life. Institutional accountability has to be dealt with seriously, because the church is part of society's institutions. The latter are not ends but means. It is impossible, for example, to do evangelism in contemporary Latin America and not deal with the reality of institutions. Whenever Jesus Christ is named there is present, in the background, the institutional church as a traditional ally of the state and the army. Likewise in the USA the name of Jesus Christ is tied up with the institution of religion, which is, in turn, tied up with the economic, political and social system.

If we are to think critically from the perspective of the kingdom of God, if we are to grow in our lifestyle, we must begin to ask ourselves: How do we incarnate, *i.e.*, how do we actualize the love, justice and peace of the kingdom in the world of institutions —in relation to the problems of education and government, of policy-making bodies and multinational corporations, of the armaments race and the ecological chaos that characterize western society?

CHRISTIANS AS SACRAMENTS   Third, we are called to grow in our lifestyle *because of what we can become*. We can become sacraments of God's kingdom.

A sacrament is a sign, something that points to a reality beyond itself. Christians are called to be a living sacrament, pointing to Jesus Christ. We are called to point with our lives and actions to the reality of God's presence in history. Christians have been made a new creation. Our status as firstfruits of God's new creation makes us a people of the future, a community *in via*. Jesus said, "Let your light so shine before men that they may see your good works."

Christians can become a "good news" people, a walking message. I say "Christians can become" because they have not always been a walking message, a good news people, a sacramental sign. Throughout history they have been, more often than we would like to admit, counter-signs, counter-messages, anti-gospel. The only way we can become what God wants us to be is by growing in Jesus Christ, by letting ourselves be "rooted and built up in him and established in the faith" (Col. 2:6, 7). Thus we will be able to "put on the new nature, which is being renewed in knowledge after the image of its creator" (Col. 3:10). The Westminster Catechism begins by asking: "What is the chief end of man?" It answers: "To glorify God and enjoy him forever."

When we call people to faith in Jesus Christ, we are not calling them to escape from reality, but rather to become a a celebrating people. By demonstrating the gospel, Christians can motivate others to worship the living God. They can enable men, women and children, entire families and nations, to fulfill their purpose in creation: to glorify God.

We Protestants talk very little about liturgy. We tend to be activists and lose sight of the "what for" of our action. I've learned a lot in dealing with Orthodox and Roman Catholics, who keep raising the question of the relationship of liturgy to evangelism. They rightly sense a closeness between worship and witness. It is to this I refer when I state that we can become instruments of worship, that we can become a sacramental community. When our lives irradiate the gospel, our good works become a call to worship. Through our lives we announce our faith and call women and men to respond to the God who has spoken and speaks.

Are we experiencing growth in the way we live? For the Christian the question of identity has to do with who has control of his or her life. If Jesus Christ is in us and we are in him; if we are experiencing the power of his resurrection (which is not the power of grandioseness and arrogant triumphalism but of humble and committed service), then women, men and children will see our good works and give glory to the Father.

CHAPTER V

MISSION
AS LIBERATION

Mission must be visible, demonstrable, verifiable. Hence the importance that the Gospels attach to Jesus' "mighty deeds" as signs of his proclamation and disciple-making functions. Those signs were not just reinforcements of his missionary message. Rather they pointed beyond themselves to God's ultimate purpose for humankind. At the same time, they revealed God's commitment to the weak and downtrodden.

One place where this is made explicit is in Luke's version of Jesus' mission. Luke tells us that Jesus chose his own local synagogue, in the village of Nazareth, to outline the nature of his mission.

And he came to Nazareth, where he had been brought up; and he went to the synagogue, as his custom was, on the sabbath day. And he stood up to read; and there was given to him the book of the prophet Isaiah. He opened the book and found the place where it was written, "The Spirit of the Lord is upon me, because he has anointed me to preach good news to the poor. He has sent me to proclaim release to the captives and recovering of sight to the blind, to set at liberty those who are oppressed, to proclaim the acceptable year of the Lord." And he closed the book, and gave it back to the attendant, and sat down; and the eyes of all in the synagogue were fixed on him. And he began to say to them, "Today this scripture has been fulfilled in your hearing." (Lk. 4:16–21)

These words have become a point of contention in the contemporary church. Some theological conservatives have criticized the way Jesus' sermon at Nazareth has been taken out of context in some activist circles and interpreted as a sociopolitical program. Socially conscious scholars and church leaders have criticized traditional exegetes for spiritualizing the words of Jesus and concealing the specific historical interpretation that Luke gives to these words.

Be that as it may, it cannot be denied that this passage places Jesus' understanding of his mission in the perspective of liberation. Whether it is understood in purely "spiritual" or sociopolitical terms, or both, is not important at this point. What is important is that we recognize the fundamental role that the language of liberation plays in Jesus' interpretation of his mission.

If we take seriously the intrinsic relation between Christ and his church, we see the importance of his inaugural sermon at Nazareth for the church's mission today. I would like to underscore two items in it.

REDISCOVERING THE LANGUAGE OF LIBERATION

There is first the fact of the rediscovery of the language of liberation. The concept of liberation is not new to the Bible. In a sense, it can be found in it from beginning to end since the Bible is concerned with the history of God's liberating deeds. Up to recently, however, the word *liberation* had remained largely dormant or at least hidden behind other words such as salvation, redemption, reconciliation and regeneration. Not until the word began to be used in a socioethical context did the church rediscover its biblical roots. In fact, so close are the ties between liberation and social action that we are forced to see the former in terms of the church's concern for a more just and humane world.

From its beginning, the modern missionary movement, whatever its theology, has served men and women's social needs. Whether it was Bartolomé de las Casas in Chiapas, Mexico, fighting for the rights of the Indians; the early Moravian missionaries, in Saint Thomas, making themselves slaves in order to minister to the black population, or in Surinam, setting up "fraternal communities" where slaves were treated as free persons, their bodies healed and their minds educated; William Carey, in Bengal, India, founding schools for boys *and* girls and making significant contributions to the advance of Bengali language and culture; Albert Schweitzer, establishing a hospital in the heart of Africa; or Susan and Harry Strachan, in Costa Rica, founding an orphanage and the first modern hospital in the country—Catholic and Protestant missionaries have seen, by and large, the improvement of life as part of their responsibility.

Not only in traditional mission lands, known today as the developing Third World, but also in Europe and North America, the church has seen the alleviation of society's ills as part of its mission involvement. Many of the educational institutions in those continents are due to early efforts of the church. The struggle for the abolition of slaves, women's and children's rights, prison reforms, humane treatment of the mentally ill and improved conditions for industrial laborers are all honorable parts of the church's heritage. Health and welfare programs for society's poor and downtrodden have taken up large shares of the church's overall energies. The various streams of the Wesleyan Movement in Britain and North America, the revival, social gospel and, more recently, the civil rights movements in the USA, the worker priest movement in France during the 1940s, the Christian labor movement in Europe and Canada and the city-mission movements in Britain, Germany and the USA have not only revealed a church concerned with the plight of the downtrodden, but have stirred up the conscience of society in general.

As far as the Third World is concerned, the church's involvement in the alleviation of social ills has run alongside the process of colonial and imperial expansion. In a real sense, the missions functioned as a social and ideological arm of the colonial and imperial powers. Although in the early stages of the modern Protestant missionary movement the missions were seen by the government mercantile companies as a threat, it was not long until they were able to come to an understanding. Thus schools, hospitals, orphanages, small-scale industry, agricultural development projects, and so forth were left to the missions in Asia, Africa, Oceania and the Caribbean. In Latin America, the mission outpost, with schools and land administration, was a constituent part of the colonial era. When Protestant missions entered in the nineteenth century, they came as the religious partner of the liberal-capitalistic movement. They were thus able to found schools, hospitals and orphanages and set up agricultural projects, since that was part of the role ascribed to them by many of the national governments and the cultural milieu of which missions were part.

Time does not allow me to consider the problems and issues involved in such an alliance. I would simply point out that for all the good of the social institutions the missions have been able to found, and for all the services they have been able to render, the negative impact which this alliance has had upon the younger churches, their members and the nations of which they are part has been far greater than what many of us would like to admit.

A case in point, with which I am historically linked, is that of my own country, Puerto Rico. It is a well-known fact that the first Protestant missionaries came to the island with the military forces of the USA during the Spanish-American War in 1898. From the first forty-two years of North American occupation, Puerto Rico suffered the impact of so-called "negative imperialism." The USA turned the island into a sugar colony and worried little about the pathetic social and economic situation of its inhabitants. Had it not been for the missions, and the churches they founded, the majority of islanders would have starved to death. Many in fact did. The missions founded hospitals and schools. They distributed clothes, food and medicine. They became the chief relief agencies in the island. Yet, for all the good they accomplished, recent historical research has underscored the fact that they also became ideological tools of the colonial power. During the first thirty years of mission work the independent aspirations of islanders began to dwindle, the movement toward statehood emerged and, worst of all, Puerto Ricans began to lose their strong national identity in favor of a diffuse "American colonial" identity. Today, to be a follower of the independence cause is to be identified with a lost, unrealistic cause; it is to be an idealistic dreamer or a no-good communist. Even worse is the way the churches have practically sold their souls to "the American way of life," so that practically all mainline churches are organizationally part of North American ecclesiastical bodies and the greatest heresy one can fall into is to opt for the cause of national liberation. Clergy persons may speak out on political issues and participate in political parties as long as they do *not* favor independence. In consequence, it would seem that the only way a church leader can express political commitment is either to be on the side of one of the two alternatives that favors the continuous submission of Puerto Rico to the USA (statehood or "commonwealth"), or—functionally, if not formally—to leave the church. For those of us who are committed to a ministry within and through the church, and are nevertheless committed to the liberation of Puerto Rico from the colonial rule of the USA, the only option available seems to be a self-imposed ecclesial exile.

The church's social ministries, however, have not developed without internal tensions. From the early days of the modern Protestant missionary movement, there have been debates among missionary societies, their missionaries and the sending churches as to whether social action is a proper task of missionary service. Some have justified it on the grounds that it was a preparation for the gospel. Some emphasized that the establishment of education, medical and social institutions was a means for building strong churches. Others, like John Mott and the Laymen's Foreign Mission Inquiry, argued that it was all part of "the larger evangelism," by which was meant the bringing of the good news to bear upon all dimensions of life. Whatever the argument, however, the fact was that the missions and churches could not turn their face from human needs. The practical reality of poverty, disease and ignorance, coupled with the compassion of the gospel, pushed them into the social service arena.

After World War II and the dismantling of the western colonial empire, the challenge of development came before the churches. The emerging nations of Africa, Asia and the Caribbean, along with their Latin American counterparts, began to realize that they were sandwiched in between two developed blocks and that if they were to survive as nations and people they would have to put every energy into economic development. Later on they discovered that their backwardness and under-development was not just a matter of economics, but also had political, social and cultural implications. What they needed was integral development. Since the missions and their ecclesial off-spring had been pioneers in these areas of service, the new governments did not hesitate to enlist their cooperation. Missions and other church agencies became key instruments, though not the only nor the major ones, in the process of development. In some European countries, like the Netherlands and West Germany, they not only confronted their governments with their responsibility to work toward the development of poor countries, but they became direct intermediaries in the allocation of financial and technical aid from their respective governments for health, agricultural and community development projects. The church's mission, especially in Africa and Asia, began to be interpreted in terms of "nation building." Development aid commanded a great amount of the energies of the churches and the missions.

During the sixties, it became increasingly obvious that such efforts were proving less and less effective for two basic reasons. On the one hand, the development programs had not been able to go to the root of the problem. While the majority of Third World nations had become independent, they were still economically, politically and culturally dependent on the developed nations. On the other hand, most of the international aid organizations were linked with the centers of world power. In consequence, they recommended "solutions" that would not harm or challenge the basic structures of international trade, or, especially, the situation of the local oligarchies, who served as allies of the rich countries. It became obvious that what was needed in the poor countries was more just and humane structures, and this called for fundamental changes at the national and international levels.

The churches, especially those who participated in the ecumenical movement, began to recognize the need for profound structural changes. Thus, at the 1966 World Conference on Church and Society it was stated:

> While most of the developing nations have achieved formal political independence, many find that they are still economically dependent on the developed nations. And such dependence has tended to inhibit both economic and political development. It has also given rise to a widespread concern for rapid social change and reform among many of the peoples of Africa, Asia and Latin America. Therefore, a second generalization can be made: a revolutionary mood pervades the thought of many active and influential groups in public life in many nations of the "Third World" and is an important factor in their politics. These groups seek national independence, not simply in the formal political sense but in the wider sense which includes economic, social and cultural factors as well. They are concerned to reduce substantially dependence on and exploitation by the developed nations. They seek economic development—by which is meant industrialization, technological advance and diversification of production—but at the same time they are concerned to promote equally fundamental changes in the organization of political and economic power, in order to enable the common man—workers, peasants, the emerging middle classes, students, and intellectuals, etc.—to share more equally in national life.[1]

A year later, Pope Paul published his encyclical, *Populorum Progressio,* in which he called for development based on a more just and humane order.[2] The growing sociopolitical awareness on the part of the church and ecumenical organizations led to concentration on efforts of "development with social justice."[3] This involved at first the promotion of decisive action for development at three levels: in developing nations, in the developed nations and in international political structures through educational and service programs. The key here was to awaken the conscience of individuals, organizations and power structures to the need for fundamental changes in the development process. Further on, it was decided that not only must the churches seek to educate for an all-out, decisive action for development, but that they should participate directly in development programs that would attack the problem at its roots and promote liberation from the chains that enslave and exploit the world's poor nations.

A terminological (and conceptual) pilgrimage has thus taken place in our decade in regard to the churches' responses to the ills of society. In *To Break the Chains of Oppression*, this pilgrimage is characterized along three basic lines.

The first is the more traditional line, which concentrates on *service:* "programs of aid, relief, construction of hospitals, clinics, schools, and other institutions which provide employment for the workers, and to those who cannot find a job."[4]

The second aims at *social reform* by the improvement of the conditions of the least privileged. Those who follow this line of action have undertaken "programs of community organization, cooperatives and mass education designed to bring about change at the local level, in the hope that such change might possibly promote or even accelerate change at the national level."[5]

The third line puts the accent on *liberation* as a collective process which seeks to overcome the structures of domination and dependence. It holds that "in order to attain development understood as social justice, self-reliance and economic growth, it is necessary to overcome the obstacles which oppose it, including anything which creates situations of dependence, national or international, for this implies the exercise of some form of domination over the dependents." This line insists, moreover, that it is "practically impossible to achieve development while there are oppressors and oppressed. There may be economic growth, but it will benefit mainly, or exclusively, the dominators at the cost of the dependents."[6]

These three lines of action, which represent both stages in the process of the churches' participation in the struggle for social justice and existing approaches toward the problems of poverty, backwardness and underdevelopment, are not without their respective flaws. The problem with the traditional line is that it limits itself to programs that remain superficial. It functions more as a tranquilizer than as an effective alternative to society's ills.

The problem with the second is that the reforms it effects tend to stay at the local level, concentrating on intermediate changes which in the long run do not bring about effective transformation at national and international levels.

The problem with the third is that so emphasizes the global struggle for liberation that it forgets that, while that struggle goes on, there are hungry people to feed, sick persons to heal, illiterates to teach, local communities to organize and empower, sexist and racist battles to fight. In other words, tranquilizers may be inadequate as long term solutions, but they certainly are necessary until the real solution is available. Local reforms may be inadequate for an overall strategy of liberation, but they can be steppingstones for overcoming national and international structures of injustice. By the same token, a global liberation process may sound too utopian, unrealizable and unpractical for the churches to spend their energies on. Yet such a goal is essential if their other diaconal actions are to have any meaning. Otherwise, the churches would be resigning themselves to a fatalistic view of history, where the poor and disenfranchised are condemned to be poorer and more wretched, and the rich and powerful, mightier and wealthier. That this cannot be an acceptable alternative for God's people is evident by a careful study of Jesus' message of liberation.

REINTERPRETING
THE MESSAGE OF LIBERATION

The rediscovery of the language of liberation has led to a new awareness as far as the biblical vision of the human is concerned. In his critique of the word *development* for obscuring "the theological problem implied in the process designated by this term," Gustavo Gutiérrez has said that "the word *liberation* allows for another approach leading to the Biblical sources which inspire the presence and action of man in history." He goes on to state that:

> In the Bible Christ is presented as the one who brings us liberation. Christ the savior liberates man from sin, which is the ultimate root of all disruption of friendship and of all injustice and oppression. Christ makes man truly free, that is to say, he enables man to live in communion with him and this is the basis for all human brotherhood.[7]

Jesus' inaugural sermon must be seen in this perspective. The entire discourse breathes an atmosphere of liberation: it announces the good news of salvation to the poor, the restoration of sight to the blind, release to the captives and freedom to the oppressed. What makes this a liberating passage is the reference to the year of Jubilee. In the Old Testament, the Jubilee was the culmination of the sabbath years. Just as every six days there was to be a day of rest, so every six years there was to be a rest throughout the land. The year of Jubilee occurred every forty-nine years, or in other words, every six sabbath years. It included, in addition to all the regular sanctions of the sabbath year, the restoration of all property to the original owners, the remission of all debts and the release of all slaves. The Jubilee, however, was hardly kept throughout the history of Israel. (This is one reason why God sent Israel into captivity.) The Jubilee, therefore, was a live issue in the prophetic literature, appearing both as a denunciation from God and as an indispensable part of the messianic promises (Ezeh. 45:7–9; 46:17–18). André Trocmé and John Howard Yoder, among others, have demonstrated that the proclamation of the year of Jubilee was no passing reference in Jesus' ministry but a central theme of his teaching.[8]

We must see Jesus' message of liberation, therefore, in an eschatological perspective. In proclaiming the "year of grace," Jesus announced the coming of a new age, an age in which love would triumph over greed, light over darkness, freedom over enslavement and hope over despair. Jesus was announcing the birth of a just and peaceful world. He opened up the horizons of history, challenging the fatalism and legalism of the prevailing Jewish system. He said that the Old Testament promises were coming to pass and that his presence at Nazareth was a fulfillment of those promises. Jesus identified himself as the promised Messiah who would bring God's liberation.

The content of this liberation is signified by three categories of people: the poor, the blind and the captives and oppressed.

Although in the Old Testament tradition, *the poor* came to signify both the pious of the Lord (that is, those who opened themselves to the Lord and waited upon him) as well as those who were deprived of the basic essentials of life, overwhelming attention is concentrated on the latter. For example, of approximately 235 references in the Old Testament where the five leading terms for the poor may be found *(ebyon, dal, ani, anaw, rash)*, only twenty-five can be identified with "poverty of spirit," or "meekness." Thus the poor are referred to sixty-one times as "beggars" *(ebyon);* forty-eight times as "weak ones" *(dal);* eighty times as "bent-over ones" *(ani);* twenty-five times as "those who humble themselves before God" *(anaw);* and twenty-one times as "indigent or needy" *(rash).* That emphasis seems to be retained in the New Testament, at least with the most frequently used term, *ptochos,* which means the "wretched ones." This word appears thirty-four times and only on six occasions does it refer to "spiritual poverty."[9]

This quantitative evidence shows *at least* that the Bible takes seriously those who are materially poor. Those who are socially, economically and politically marginated, who are powerless because they are deprived of basic essentials of life, are said to have God on their side. Their condition is a scandal and an insult to the God who created humankind in his image, to live in community and look after one another.

The poor disclose profound dimensions of God's relationship with humanity. We see in God's solidarity with the poor *the depth of his justice,* which uplifts the fallen and cares for the bruised. We see in the poor the path through which humankind must travel in order to be reconciled to God; only those who humble themselves before God, who open themselves to him, who trust not in themselves nor in their material possessions, who adapt the "spirit" of the poor, can find favor in God's sight.[10]

The *blind* represent the physically handicapped, those deprived of the normal functions of their bodies. Their condition is a physical evidence of sin's effect upon the human body: how it has deterred and deformed God's creation. Yet there is more to it than what is readily apparent, for the blind are not just the physically ill. The blind are also the Gentiles, who lack the light of God's revelation. They are Israel, who having had it, has distorted it. The blind are thus a symbol of the distortion that sin has brought about both in the body and in the human moral and religious conscience. In our day, we would venture to add those who suffer from what the Indonesians call "letter-blindness"— illiteracy and lack of education in general.

Within the concept of the year of Jubilee, the *captives and oppressed* were those who had fallen into slavery because of inability to pay their debts. In one of the two verses quoted by Jesus in his inaugural sermon, Isaiah 58:6, this is certainly the idea. In the passage from which this verse is taken, the prophet denounces the people for not keeping the provisions of the Jubilee.[11] But in the other passage, Isaiah 61:1-2, the reference is to the future definitive gathering of the messianic people, when the Gentiles shall be converted to Israel's God and a new Jerusalem shall rise in glory.

It seems to me that in his sermon Jesus was referring both to those who were financially indebted *then and there* and thus had been put into jail,[12] and also to the *future* gathering of the people of God in the eschaton. Jesus affirms that he has been sent "to *proclaim* release to the captives" (a phrase borrowed from Isaiah 61:1-2). He is announcing a future hope that is not yet within his power to fulfill. When the disciples, for example, asked him about the restoration of "the kingdom to Israel," he answered that it was not for them "to know times or seasons which the Father has fixed by his own authority" (Acts 1:6-7). In other words, the ultimate manifestation of the kingdom is the sole responsibility of the Father—although through the resurrection he has given the Son the task of bringing it about in due course. Meanwhile, however, Jesus limits himself to proclaiming that day, and commissions his disciples to do likewise.

In the other case, however, Jesus affirms his determination to set free the oppressed (a phrase he borrows from Isaiah 58:6). As he also taught his disciples to pray, "forgive us our sins, for we ourselves forgive everyone who is indebted to us" (Lk. 11:4). John Howard Yoder comments that in this model prayer, "which summarizes the thought of Jesus concerning prayer, . . . Jesus is not simply recommending vaguely that [his disciples] might pardon those who have bothered [them] or made [them] trouble, but tells [them] purely and simply to erase the debts of those who owe [them] money; which is to say, practice the Jubilee."[13]

The liberation which Jesus brings is both future and present. Future, because it awaits the ultimate fulfillment of the kingdom, the moment when God shall wipe away all tears, when "death shall be no more, neither shall there be mourning nor crying nor pain any more, for the former things" will have passed away and God will have made "all things new" (Rev. 21:4-5). It is also a liberation for the here and now. First, because the prelude of what is to come is already taking place in the forgiveness that is effected in everyone who repents and believes in the name of Jesus, and in the demand to forgive the debts of their debtors, which accompanies the experience of forgiveness. In other words, the ultimate liberation finds its "first fruits" in the freedom which Jesus gives from human greed and egoism, and in the command to set free those who are indebted to us. Since followers of Christ have been set free from all the "gods of this world," especially material possessions, they are now free, indeed they are commanded, to set free those who have come under their dominion.

Second, the liberation which Christ brings is a present reality because of the other liberating signs that have started to appear before everyone's eyes. When John the Baptist sent his disciples to ask Jesus whether he was the one who was to come or should he look for another, Jesus responded with concrete deeds: "he cured many of diseases and plagues and evil spirits, and on many that were blind he bestowed sight" (Lk. 7:21). Then, *after* he had done these things, he told them what to say to John:

> Go and tell John what you have seen and heard: the blind receive their sight, the lame walk, lepers are cleansed, and the deaf hear, the dead are raised up, the poor have good news preached to them. And blessed is he who takes no offense at me. (Lk. 7:22–23)

Because the liberation that Jesus brings is not just a future hope, but a present possibility, therefore, it is given as a charge to the church. In a text that some may be tempted to disregard because it is not found in the earliest manuscripts, but which, nevertheless, captures and interprets faithfully the teaching of the Gospel of Mark, we find Jesus saying:

> Go into all the world and preach the gospel to the whole creation. He who believes and is baptized will be saved; but he who does not believe will be condemned. And these signs will accompany those who believe: in my name they will cast out demons; they will speak in new tongues; they will pick up serpents, and if they drink any deadly thing, it will not hurt them; they will lay their hands on the sick, and they will recover. (Mk. 16:15–18)

The thing I wish to point out is not the seeming "exoticism" of these signs: the casting out of demons, the speaking in new tongues, the picking up of serpents, the drinking of poison without being harmed and the healing of the sick by the imposition of hands. I am simple enough to believe that all of those things can take place in our day. But they are not the main thrust of this passage. Rather its message is the affirmation that the church's mission does not take place in a vacuum but in a context of liberation. The word the church has been entrusted to proclaim and teach must be accompanied, authenticated, by what Paul called the "demonstration of the Spirit and of power" (1 Cor. 2:4).

Jesus' sermon is introduced by a reference to the Spirit. "The Spirit of the Lord is upon me . . ." According to Luke, Jesus had just returned from the desert "in the power of the Spirit." (Lk. 4:14). In that context, the Spirit is shown as the force that enables Jesus to fulfill his mission ("he has anointed me to . . ."). The Spirit's anointing encompasses not only the proclamation of good news to the poor and liberation to the captives, but also the restoration of sight to the blind and the setting at liberty of the oppressed. All of those acts are signs of the messianic era, "the acceptable year of the Lord." It is in the concrete manifestations of these signs that we must understand the meaning of being "filled with the Holy Spirit."

The message of liberation in Jesus Christ cannot be limited to the proclamation of the gospel, not even to the teaching of "the whole counsel of God" (Acts 20:27). The message needs the accompanying signs that Jesus is said to have promised the disciples who would follow, those who would believe in his name. Paul testified to the Roman church:

> For I will not venture to speak of anything except what Christ has wrought through me to win obedience from the Gentiles, by word and deed, by the power of signs and wonders, by the power of the Holy Spirit, so that from Jerusalem and as far round as Illyricum I have fully preached the gospel of Christ. (Rom. 15:18–19)

We don't know exactly what deeds accompanied Paul's mission to the Gentiles, but from the witness of Luke, in Acts, and from Paul's own writings we can get a fairly good idea. They included his prophetic authority against the powers of darkness; his concern for the poor, especially the poor of Jerusalem, the orphans and widows; his courage in the face of trouble and his self-sacrifice for the well-being of others; his capacity to love even his enemies, his commitment to a new society without distinction of class, race or sex, yet his ability to adapt himself to and endure the burdens of the existing order; and his prophetic witness to the State. In our day, the liberating signs of the gospel would have to include participation in the human struggles against economic and political imperialism, mental and physical infirmities, the ills of ignorance, poverty and hunger and of racial and sexual discrimination. It would also have to involve the quest for cultural identity; and, especially, the battles against the systematic violation of the fundamental rights of men and women and against the pollution and destruction of the environment.

The church of Jesus Christ has been inflicted in our day by a diabolic polarization in its missional program. Christians, missionary organizations and movements, church and ecumenical bodies, have been spending endless energies arguing among themselves about whether their missional programs should include teaching and preaching the gospel or engaging in the sociopolitical liberation of the weak and oppressed, or both; whether the gospel should be in word or in deed only, or in word *and* deed. This is as useless a debate as it is a senseless and satanic waste of time, energies and resources.

The true test of mission is not whether we proclaim, make disciples or engage in social, economic and political liberation, but whether we are capable of integrating all three in a comprehensive, dynamic *and consistent* witness. We need to pray that the Lord will liberate us not only *from* this stagnant situation, but that he may liberate us *for* wholeness and integrity in mission.

THE GOSPEL
AND THE POOR

Over the last several years, theologians have paid increasing attention to the place of the poor in the gospel. In one of the most recent studies on this subject, Julio de Santa Ana states that "the poverty and misery in which millions of the inhabitants of our planet lie" is one of "the most dramatic signs that can be taken notice of in a reading of the facts of our time."[1] He then goes on to deal with the challenge posed by the existence of the sociologically poor to those "who profess biblical faith and believe in Jesus Christ as God and Savior in accordance with the Scriptures."[2]

Nearly two-thirds of humankind are deprived of the essentials of life. The reason why this constitutes a problem for Christians is, as noted already in the previous chapter, that the Scriptures in general and the gospel in particular are undeniably concerned with the situation of the poor. The gospels not only point out Jesus' personal poverty, for instance, but also emphasize his ministry to those rejected by society. In this, the gospels verify Paul's assertion that although the Lord Jesus Christ "was rich, yet for [our] sake he became poor, so that by his poverty [we] might become rich" (2 Cor. 8:9). And again: "though he was in the form of God, [he] did not count equality with God a thing to be grasped, but emptied himself, taking the form of a servant, being born in the likeness of men" (Phil. 2:6–7).

This stress on poverty in the life and ministry of Jesus coincides with the social teaching of the OT, where the poor occupy a privileged place, and with the poverty program of the early church (e.g., the community of goods depicted in the early chapters of Acts; with the special attention given to widows; with the concern for the poor of Jerusalem reflected in Paul's collection; the insistence on social equality (i.e., on a relation of mutual love and acceptance) in the gathered community of faith and in the personal relationship between believers; and with James' stern denunciation for the oppression of the poor by the rich in the church). Little wonder that the gospel writers take such care to bring out special anecdotes and parables underlying the special relationship between the good news of the kingdom and the poor of the earth. Luke in fact goes as far as stating that they are the heirs of the kingdom: "Blessed are you poor, for yours is the kingdom of God" (Lk. 6:21).

Herman Ridderbos, while arguing that in Scripture "the concept 'poor' is determined both socially and in a religious ethical sense" as those who are sociologically oppressed and wait upon the Lord for their salvation, insists that this refers specifically to the Covenant People of God and not to every human being.[3] From this, it follows by inference that the religioethical sense has priority over the sociological.

Ridderbos' treatment of the "poor" texts in the Gospels and Psalms leaves one with some reservations as to his readiness to accept the author's original intention. For example, his ready assumption that Luke uses the term *ptochos* in 4:18, 6:20 and 7:22 as the equivalent of Matthew's "poor in spirit" (Mt. 5:5), by which he bypasses the peculiar interest of Lucan theology on the physical, and the fact that "no less than five of the nine complexes in which Luke uses *ptochos* are peculiar to the author,"[4] leaves one with the impression that this respectable Dutch scholar is more interested in proving his (ideological) presupposition about the poor in the kingdom than in coming to grips with the radical nature of Luke's theology of poverty. Be that as it may, Ridderbos begs the issue of the poor in Scripture when he locates them in the perspective of the Covenant. For, after all, whom do the

Covenant People *represent?* What is the *meaning* of Israel in the world of nations? Are the true people of God a *paradigm* of the new society, or are they not? What is the meaning of the privileged place assigned to the poor in the Covenant?

It seems to me that within the framework of the Covenant, the poor are important not just because of their faithfulness to God but because of his relationship with *humanity.* God's relationship with the poor reveals the redemptive quality of his justice, which restores the fallen and heals the bruised (cf. Ex. 22:21; 23:9; Lev. 19:33; Deut. 27:19). By the same token, the poor disclose the demands of the New Covenant: meekness, openness to God and trust in him alone (cf. Lk. 18:18–25). No wonder, then, that Jesus associated his mission with the poor, the blind, the captives and the oppressed—because they bear the greatest evidence of the tragedy of sin! The gospel is for all those who see themselves as broken and bruised. To them it announces the Year of Jubilee: the new age of God, yea, the liberation of history!

This is why the poor profoundly affect the identity of the church. The church is both a sign of the commitment of God's mission with the struggle of the wretched of the earth and first fruits of the new creation. In the church, there should be room for all types of human beings, but especially for the outcast, broken and marginal of society, because the church is a *paradigm* of the new humanity that God is creating through the saving work of Christ, a paradigm realized and made present by the power of the Holy Spirit out of the discordance and deformation of society. The struggle of the poor for liberation from their material oppressive situations should *also* be the church's struggle given its calling to be a priestly and prophetic community. To fulfill this task effectively, the church must embody the history of rejection, exploitation and domination of the oppressed majorities of the earth; it must participate in their present state of repressed frustrations, silent protests or overt efforts to break the chains of oppression; and it must articulate their future hopes and aspirations.

The idea that the sociologically poor occupy a privileged place in God's economy has been challenged, however, by G. D. Gort in an essay dedicated to an analysis of the place of the poor in the gospel. He questions one of the propositions attached to my doctoral dissertation (done at the Free University of Amsterdam). The proposition reads, "The gospel is particularly addressed to the poor, their struggle is a fundamental concern of God's mission and thus profoundly affects the identity of the church."[5]

Gort states "that an affirmation of this nature requires to be rejected on account of its *materialist* and *particularist* complexion."[6] He argues that to take the term *poor* as referring to the sociologically (or materially) poor is to fail to take "full account of the biblical witness regarding" the notion of rich and poor (p. 90), and to "tend toward a kind of glorification of poverty" (p. 92). Furthermore, he asserts that it implies a reduction of the biblical notion of liberation, in the sense that it limits it "to the present age alone" (p. 94) and to "only a part of the totality of human existence" (p. 95), and consequently, "a curtailment of God's saving activity." (pp. 94, 96ff.) According to him this proposition "also gives an exclusivist coloration to . . . the gospel." (p. 98) This entails (1) "a one-sided perception of the message of the Evangel" (p. 98); (2) "a basic lack of compassion" (by *excluding* from the addressees of the gospel those that are not poor and by dividing or separating humanity into two camps, the haves and the have-nots) (pp. 99, 100); and (3) a subversion "of the very thing for which it is after" (material liberation), because it fails to deal with the root of poverty (sin) for which the only solution is the personal transformation of both dominators and dominated (pp. 101, 102).

Gort has a logical basis for interpreting the word *particular* as exclusive. However, this is but *one* of several denotations and connotations of the term, which can also be understood as *special,* and in fact this *is* the way the term is used in the proposition. This is corroborated by the second clause: "Their struggle is a fundamental concern of God's mission." The use of the indefinite article before *fundamental* indicates that "the struggle of the poor" is but *one* of the concerns of God's mission. To be sure, it is a *fundamental* concern, but God has other items on his agenda. If this is so, then the first part of the proposition can only be taken in the sense of a specificity within a general thrust. To say that "the gospel is *particularly* addressed to the poor" is not to deny that it is *generally* addressed to all human beings. It is simply to underscore the special, privileged place of the sociologically poor.

Neither can the sociological character of the poor in this proposition be construed as a denial of spiritual poverty and its place in the gospel. What the proposition does imply, as noted in this exposition, is that the sociologically poor are important to the gospel not just because of their situation, but also because of their kerygmatic significance: They disclose the depth of God's justice and the path that must be followed in order to be reconciled to God; that is, adoption of the "spirit" of the poor.

In this respect, Gort has set up a straw man, since he has *read into* the proposition implications that I did not intend and that cannot possibly be deduced when the proposition is taken in its entirety. But, by so doing, Gort can make the proposition *appear* as a deformation of the gospel and, by inference,[7] present what cannot but be interpreted as a distorted picture of my own understanding of the good news of salvation. This is hardly fair and honest. One would expect a more responsible treatment from an otherwise serious scholar.

Be that as it may, Gort's argument opens itself to serious criticism at various points. For example, he claims that the proposition does not take "full account of the biblical witness" regarding the categories of "rich" and "poor." Then he goes on to assert "that Scripture taken as a whole understands [these notions] inclusively: At times they have a spiritual (figurative) meaning, sometimes a literal one, at other times an element of both" (p. 90). Then he goes to illustrate his point by exegeting the pericope of Jesus' "hard saying" regarding the camel and the eye of a needle (Mt. 19:24; Mk. 10:25; Lk. 18:25). He concludes that "the main subject of the pericope . . . is not riches or not even the *having* of things in and of itself, but rather the *hold* earthly possessions can and usually do have on a person, a hold so strong that one is no longer *at liberty* to follow the Master; possessions of whatever nature, very easily form a barrier to discipleship" (p. 92).

The proposition, however, does not deal with the rich, but with the poor. Gort would thus have to demonstrate from Scripture that the sociologically poor *do not* have a privileged place in salvation history, that they are *not* the poor of Jesus' proclamation and that they *do not* affect the church's identity. But this he fails to do. Besides, the very material Gort presents as evidence (the aforementioned pericope) confirms my argument, namely, that in order to follow Jesus one must renounce all and become like the poor (humble and totally dependent on God).

This is by no means a glorification of poverty. The Bible does not glorify poverty; it condemns it as a scandalous condition and demands justice for the poor. Precisely for this reason, God identifies himself with the poor. This is also why Jesus assumed a life of poverty and why Paul associated the preaching of the cross with the humble and ignorant (1 Cor. 1:18ff.). The gospel is a protest against the scandal of poverty and a call to eradicate it from human life. Those who respond to its message must themselves renounce any form of manipulation and oppression and commit themselves to the well-being of their neighbor. They must surrender totally to the God who in Jesus Christ has promised to liberate the world from oppression. And oppression (an obvious consequence of sin) is a fundamental cause of poverty.[8] That the gospel is a promise puts the call to repentance and faith in an eschatological perspective. The call to conversion implies not only commitment to transform the present, but also the hope that the transformation will one day truly come to pass. It is in this eschatological perspective that the proposition in question should be understood.

At bottom, Gort is concerned that the inclusiveness of the gospel not be obliterated and, therefore, that the rich not be discriminated against. He wants to underscore the psychological impoverishment of the rich and their need for liberation. He writes, of course, as a representative of the rich world and as such wants to defend its place in God's economy. Neither the proposition nor my defense *exclude* the wealthy from the offer of salvation and the call to faith and repentance (cf. pp. 103ff.). Nor does it deny the obvious psychological impoverishment of the wealthy. It merely tries to underscore the importance of the sociologically poor because they represent a scandalous condition against which the gospel is a perennial protest. In this respect, it must be said that psychological oppression cannot be understood without its sociological counterpart, just as spiritual poverty cannot be appreciated except in the context of the material.[9]

Gort seems to lose sight of the fact that, while according to biblical revelation "all have sinned" and are poverty stricken before God (Ro. 3:23), sin is not an abstract reality but takes concrete form. Sin expresses itself historically in the failure of human beings to relate with one another on the basis of love, or in more positive terms, in the oppression of men and women by their neighbors.[10] This is why the OT states emphatically that to know God is to do justice (Jer. 22:13–16), a notion that is taken up in the NT, especially by John (cf. 1 Jn. 3:7). Hence it must be dealt with not only personally and subjectively, but also objectively and publicly. The cross of Christ is not just the place where our personal sins were dealt with once and for all, but is also the place where the oppressive powers of this world have been condemned to death. At the cross, says Paul (Col. 2:15), Christ "disarmed the principalities and powers and made a public example of them, triumphing over them."[11]

Whatever else may be said about the salvation of rich and poor in the Bible, one thing remains clear: Salvation comes by way of conversion from sin and self to God and neighbor. Negatively, this implies a disposition to change one's egoistic values, to renounce any pretension of self-sufficiency and to break with any form of oppression. Positively, it means commitment to God's kingdom and its righteousness, total dependence on the Lord Jesus Christ and entrance into a life of liberating service to all human beings in general and to the sociologically oppressed in particular. In this sense, it must be recognized that "while material poverty is condemned as a scandalous condition, nevertheless, it constitutes a privileged path to the poverty of the Spirit, because those who have nothing have less difficulty in humbling themselves before God, than those who have riches."[12]

The church should be affected both in its self-image and in its lifestyle by the psychological impoverishment of the rich. But it should be particularly affected by the harsh reality of a world broken and divided between a minority of haves and a majority of have-nots and by the struggle of the latter to become free from the bondage imposed on them by the sinful attitudes and behavior of the former. In this context, the church is called on to bear a direct witness against the scandal of poverty, whether in its sociological expression or in its psychological manifestation. But it can only bear this witness to the extent that it assumes the identity of the sociologically poor and lives in a spirit of humility, openness and dependence on God. In the words of Gustavo Gutiérrez:

> Only by rejecting poverty in order to protest against it can the Church preach something that is uniquely its own: "Spiritual poverty," that is, the openness of man and history to the future promised by God. Only in this way will the Church be able to fulfill authentically—and with any possibility of being listened to—its prophetic function of denouncing every injustice to man. And only in this way will it be able to preach the word which liberates, the word of genuine brotherhood.[13]

CHAPTER VI

MISSION
AS CELEBRATION

One of the most fascinating books of the Bible is the Revelation of John. The mystery and awesomeness of its language has caught the imagination of many. No other biblical book seems to be studied, loved, treasured and, regrettably, distorted more. Recent futuristic sensations, like *The Late Great Planet Earth* by Hal Lindsey, have awakened curiosity in our troubled times about the "last things."

The book of Revelation, however, is not a blueprint for the future. It is not even an outline of the stages of history. Rather it is a celebration of the Christian faith, an interpretation of God's mission at a historical crossroad—as manifested in the Roman Empire (c. A.D. 95–96) during the days of the Emperor Domitian.[1] It rises from a profound worshiping experience and missionary situation. John says he is on the island of Patmos, banned and imprisoned "on account of the word of God and the testimony of Jesus" (1:9), when he was given a vision of the risen Christ. John shares the vision with a group of churches that evidently had been part of his pastoral charge. Like him, they were in a missionary situation. They shared with him "the tribulation, the kingdom and the patient endurance" that characterize the witness to Jesus Christ and his Word.

Generally speaking, the book is structured along a threefold pattern. It starts with a vision of the triune God, with Christ as the central point of reference ("him who is and who was and who is to come . . . the seven spirits who are before his throne, and . . . Jesus Christ, the faithful witness, the first-born of the dead, and the ruler of kings on earth") (1:4). This is followed by a vision of the internal situation of the seven churches of Asia (chapters 2–3). The greater part of the book (4:1 to the end) is a vision of God's mission in history.

Chapters 4 and 5 of this last section give a global picture of the history of God's mission, from creation to consummation, in the language of worship and praise. These chapters are an "overture" to the entire section. In them, mission appears as the celebration of a dynamic reality and a comprehensive process.

CELEBRATING IN CONTEXT

Let us consider, first, the context of this breathtaking scene. John is said to have been taken to the "heavenly sanctuary," to God's abode (4:2). This is depicted as a three-layered universe, with heaven above, the earth in the middle and hell underneath. We must not let the modern scientific perspective deter us from appreciating what the seer is trying to convey. He can describe the universe only in the categories then available to him. The point of the description is that God's throne stands over human thrones. The kings of the earth, including Domitian and his entire Roman Empire, are subject to and held accountable by him. Heaven is the place where history can be observed in its density. From nowhere else are we able to get such a comprehensive vision of human history's complexities.

Following an old oriental tradition that separates each layer of the universe by a body of water, the author describes heaven as separated from the earth by a "sea of glass" (4:6). God stands over and above the nations but is not detached from their activities. Rather he keeps watch on them as through a crystal glass. No one stands outside the range of God's eyes.

Around "the throne was a rainbow" (4:3), perhaps reminding John of the covenant God had made with Noah after the flood when he promised to be merciful with humankind, and never again let "his judgment fall upon the entire race."[2] The rainbow stands as a sign of God's loving attitude toward the nations, his long-suffering and patient endurance, "not wishing that any should perish, but that all should reach repentance" (2 Pet. 3:9).

This vision took place on "the Lord's day" (1:10), when John was "in the Spirit," a reference to the fact that it happened while John was praying.

CELEBRATING IN COMMUNITY

Who are the actors in this magnificent service of worship? The one who commands most of the observer's attention is the triune God. He is disclosed in his functions within the divine plan.

The first member of the Godhead who is brought to our attention is the Father: "and lo, a throne stood in heaven, with one seated" (4:2). This *one* is linked with creation and providence. He is worshiped as "the Lord God Almighty" (4:8) who is worthy "to receive glory and honor and power," for he created "all things, and by [his] will they existed and were created" (4:11). He has effective control of history: he holds in his right hand "the scroll," signifying his authority over creation. In the words of the children's song, "He's got the whole wide world in his hands."

Standing before the throne is the Son, who is linked with redemption and consummation. It is he who introduces John into the heavenly sanctuary as "the first voice" who speaks "like a trumpet," inviting him to "come hither" (4:1). Christ thus appears as the fundamental point of reference in one's knowledge of God. It is by him that we are able to plunge into the mystery of God; through him we are able to see God. He is depicted as the Lion of Judah (the triumphant Messiah) who has prevailed over sin and death and has, therefore, the power to open "the scroll" and interpret the mystery of history (5:5). But he is also referred to as the Lamb (the suffering Servant) who was slain (5:6) and by his blood ransomed men and women for God "from every tribe and tongue and people and nation" (5:9).

Linking the ministry of Father and Son is the Holy Spirit, shown as the agent of creation, providence, redemption and consummation. He is described as "the seven spirits of God" (4:5). Biblical scholars tell us that the number *seven* stands in Apocalyptic literature for perfection or completeness. In Revelation, it is used to develop the main thoughts of the book. Thus, we have seven letters (1:1–3, 20) to seven churches (chapters 2–3), seven seals (5:1–7:17), seven trumpets (8:1–11:14), seven signs (11:15—14:20), seven bowls of wrath (15:1–16:17a), seven voices from heaven (16:17b—19:5) and seven visions of the final victory (19:11—21:4). In chapters 4 and 5, the "seven spirits" appear in reference to the faithfulness of the third member of the Godhead. The Spirit is before the Father's throne issuing "flashes of lightning, and voices and peals of thunder" (4:5), underscoring the fact that God is the "tremendous mystery" and reminiscent of "the terrible mystery . . . felt on Mount Sinai (Exodus 19:16; Ezekiel 1:13; Psalms 18:14; 50:3)" at the institution of the law.[3] But the Spirit is also described as the eyes of the Lamb (5:6), "sent out into all the earth" to continue Christ's redemptive mission in every tribe, tongue, race and nation. He is the agent of the divine activity in history: the redemptive message goes to the world and the world is brought face to face with God.[4]

John is able to give us this picture of the triune God only through symbolic images, similes and metaphors. As one commentator has said, John "ransacks the entire biblical and extrabiblical literature so that he might be able somehow to communicate to others his experience of God."[5]

There are other participants besides the members of the Godhead. What John sees is not a private show of the divine trinity, but the collective celebration of everything that lives.

There are the twenty-four elders, dressed in white robes and sitting around the throne (4:4). Interpreters disagree as to their identity.[6] George Eldon Ladd concludes, The "twenty-four elders are a company of angels who serve as a sort of heavenly counterpart to the elders of Israel (Exodus 24:11), who are pictured as helping to execute the divine rule."[7] Representing the witness of heaven to God's mighty acts in history, they worship him for what he has done in creation and providence, for the redemption he has wrought in the Son. "He is about to bring history to its goal,"[8] to judge the dead and reward his "servants, the prophets and the saints" (11:16).

There are also four living creatures with eyes in front and in back, one with the face of a lion, the second an ox, the third a man and the fourth an eagle (4:6–8; 5:8a). An ancient rabbinic saying (A.D. 300) goes like this: "The mightiest among the birds is the eagle, the mightiest among the domestic animals is the bull, the mightiest among the wild beast is the lion, and mightiest among all is man."[9] These four creatures seem to represent the most important earthly beings. If the twenty-four elders represent the witness of heaven, the four creatures are the witness of earth and nature. Their eyes in front and back seem to point to the fact that everything that lives on earth is aware of God's mighty works. They thus bear continuous witness to God's work in creation and providence. Recalling the seraphim of Isaiah 6, they sing "Holy, holy, holy is the Lord God Almighty, who was and is and is to come!" (4:8). When they hear the Lamb being praised for his work of redemption, they answer "Amen!" (5:14). Paul tells us:

> I consider that the sufferings of this present time are not worth comparing with the glory that is to be revealed to us. For the creation waits with eager longing for the revealing of the sons of God; for the creation was subjected to futility, not of its own will but by the will of him who subjected it in hope; because the creation itself will be set free from its bondage to decay and obtain the glorious liberty of the children of God. (Rom. 8:18–21)

The saints, a fourth group of participants, are depicted in a threefold way. They appear, first, as the redeemed community from every tongue, tribe, race and nation (5:9b). They are shown, second, as the praying community, whose prayers of intercessions and lamentations are contained in "golden bowls full of incense" which the twenty-four elders hold in their hands (5:8), signifying that those prayers have not gone unheard. Third, they are revealed as the witnessing community, having been made, through redemption, a people liberated (kingdom) to bear witness (priests) about the mercies of God throughout the earth (6:10; cf. 1 Pet. 2:9, 10).

The angels are the servants of the celestial court (5:2, 11). One of them announces the transition from the celebration of creation (4:1–11) to the celebration of redemption (5:2). Then "myriads of myriads and thousands of thousands" celebrate the exaltation of the Lamb: "Worthy is the Lamb who was slain, to receive power and wealth and wisdom and might and honor and glory and blessing!" (5:12).

CELEBRATING WITH MEANING

From the Christian perspective, worship is not exhausted by its ritual. Rather, everything that is said and done in worship must embody a message. What is the message of this heavenly celebration?

First, God is in control of history. He is no absentee landlord who has left his tenants to themselves, one who does not care how men and women relate personally and collectively with one another, or who has let history run its own course and every nation do its own thing. Rather, he is present in history, preserving it from chaos and bringing it to its final goal: judging the nations in righteousness, creating a new humanity, and transforming the existing order.

The difference between John of Patmos and other Apocalyptists of his day was that he was neither pessimist nor escapist. For him evil would not triumph over good, death over life, love over hate, Satan over Christ, the kingdoms of this world over the kingdom of God. Rather, good would overcome evil, love would overshadow hate, Christ would prevail over Satan, the kingdom of God would overrule the kingdoms of this world.

Because God is in control, the Christian church need not flee from history's conflicts. It should not be afraid of human lords and emperors. It should not give way to the temptation of wanting to escape from the tribulations that come along in the fulfillment of its mission. It should rather see itself as a community called to engagement in the crossroads of life. Since it has been set free by the Lamb, it should freely plunge and immerse itself in his service in the arena of history, where God is involved in redemption and judgment.

Second, mission is a comprehensive and dynamic process. It involves the missional action of the Spirit, moving to-and-fro in the world, pointing to the Lamb and eliciting responses of faith and adoration from the human family. This activity is comprehensive in that the Spirit uses many witnesses and leaves no area of life unaffected. It is dynamic in that he is not bound to any one method or pattern of action, but rather moves in the freedom of his own mysterious ways.

In the last several years I have had to cope on more than one occasion with the surprises of the Spirit. One of the greatest is to have learned, to my shame, that members of the Orthodox Church are not only interested in evangelism, but are themselves dynamically engaged in sharing their faith with others. Why, I was taught that members of this church were "deadwood"; that they were more interested in their "mysterious ceremonies" than in naming the name of Christ; that they were bound to a static, anti-missionary tradition and were imprisoned in cultural ghettoes! My attitude revealed a blind spot, the fruit of my ignorance about the missional reality of Orthodoxy in many countries.

In 1973, at an Evangelism Symposium sponsored by the Commission on World Mission and Evangelism of the World Council of Churches, I first saw and heard an Indian Syrian Orthodox priest, bearded, wearing a long black robe and speaking in what seemed to me a weird language. The first thing that came to my mind was, what on earth was this guy doing there in a meeting on evangelism. Then, as I heard him share his evangelistic experiences in South India, witnessing to Hindus about Jesus, the light and Savior of the world; as I knelt down in prayer with him and heard him pray for the millions around the world who were without personal knowledge of Christ; when I became aware of his courageous stand against poverty and injustice and his equally strong commitment for the proclamation and celebration of the gospel in his own cultural, anti-Christian environment, I sensed what Peter must have sensed at Cornelius's house, when he and his companions saw that the Holy Spirit had fallen upon Gentiles. The Christian mission is full of surprises because it is the province of the Spirit.

Third, worship is intrinsically related to God's action in history and the conversion of the nations to God. Worship in its human dimension rises from mission. It is a spontaneous result of the experience of redemption. By the same token, mission should be seen as a worshiping event. It celebrates what God has done for women and men in Jesus Christ. It calls them to receive and share the gift of God's grace.[10]

There is no dichotomy between worship and mission. Worship is the gathering of the people sent into the world to celebrate what God has done in Christ and is doing through their participation in the spirit's witnessing action. Mission is the culmination and anticipation of worship. In worship and mission the redeemed community gives evidence to the fact that it is a praying and a witnessing people.

Yet in our churches we may have given the impression that worship and mission do not belong together, that they are opposite concerns, that they are not two dimensions of a single reality. Some have even gone as far as saying that a centrifugal, going, missionary church cannot be also a centripetal, coming, liturgical community. This is both theological non-sense and a practical fallacy. Liturgy without mission is like a river without a spring. Mission without worship is like a river without a sea. Both are necessary. Without the one, the other loses its vitality and meaning. Put in other terms, the test of a vigorous worship experience will be a dynamic participation in mission. The test of a faithful missional involvement will be a profound worship experience.

Fourth, the God who is Lord of history is the God of the cross. He wants to be remembered by his pierced hands and feet, as the slain Lamb and the suffering Servant. Having prevailed over sin and death by the resurrection, he reveals himself as the crucified God[11] who has taken sides with the weak and outcast. Therefore, the book of Hebrews describes Christ's death as having taken place outside the gates of the city,[12] where the non-persons of society must find their dwelling.

The Lord of history reveals his power in the weakness of his death. Paul tells us that "God chose what is weak in the world to shame the strong" (1 Cor. 1:27). He chose to reveal his saving power through the foolishness of the cross. Crucified in weakness, Jesus "lives by the power of God" (2 Cor. 13:4). Made alive by his resurrection from the dead, he has chosen the simple, the poor and disenfranchised to reveal "the power of God and the wisdom of God" (1 Cor. 1:26–28, 24). Having brought them into his unshakable kingdom, he calls them to go forth to him "outside the camp," to "bear the abuse he endured" (Heb. 13:13). The reference is not to suffering for one's personal faith but rather for one's commitment to others' well-being. It is in weakness that God makes us strong. It is in giving that we receive; it is in dying that we live (Francis of Assisi).

The Christian church in the North Atlantic during the last quarter of the twentieth century has been having to come to terms with the implications of the cross for its participation in God's mission. After centuries of triumphal theologies of glory, with the accent on the victorious Lion of Judah and glorious visions of a mighty, all-powerful, conquering foreign missionary movement, the western church has been having to swallow the bitter herbs of the breaking-down of Christendom, the resurgence of other religions and religious movements, the shutting up of many mission fields and the feeling of inertia that has overtaken many Christians in local congregations.

In its crisis, a true state of spiritual agony, it has begun to discover that the victorious Lion is the slain Lamb. It is having to realize that its greatest glory does not lie in the marvelous works it is able to perform: not in the millions of dollars it is able to raise for the cause of mission, nor in the thousands of young people it is able to recruit for service in the world's remote parts, nor in the fabulous reports they will be able to send back home. Rather, its glory will lie on the cross of Christ. Its greatest merit will be the sensitivity it is able to develop toward the leading of the Spirit, its openness to his mysterious ways. Its greatest achievement will be marked by its ability to serve humbly in collaboration with the thousands of churches and millions of Christians whom the Holy Spirit is raising among the weak and disenfranchised of the earth—without fanfare, without financial resources and without academically qualified personnel.

Mission is God's gift. It is the process by which God has given, gives and will continue to give himself to his creation. Mission has its origin and foundation in the circle of love of the divine Trinity. It has manifested itself in creation, in God's providential care and in Christ's redemptive work. It will culminate with Christ's bringing history to its final goal and rushing in new heavens and a new earth.

Mission is thus a cause for celebration, and we should celebrate it in humility, with gratitude, and confidently.

We should celebrate it in humility because we are only part of what God is doing around the world. We are not even the most important part; the Spirit of God is the chief executive of God's mission. We are no more than a junior partner.

We should celebrate God's mission with gratitude because, although we are not the sole or most important partner, God has given us the privilege of participating in such a marvelous way that he uses our limited services and transforms them into instruments of his grace. We may fail and fall short of his expectations, but Jesus remains faithful. He is "the same yesterday and today and forever." (Heb. 13:8). Our witness may be weak and shaky, but God's Word "shall not return [to him] empty, but . . . shall accomplish that which [he has purposed], and prosper in the thing for which [he] sent it" (Is. 55:11).

We should celebrate God's mission in the confidence of the gospel. For we have been made "a kingdom and priests." We should dare to participate in God's mission in the certain hope that our praises and our prayers will be "sweet offerings" unto the Lord.

> To him who sits upon the throne and to the Lamb be blessing and honor and glory and might for ever and ever! AMEN! (Rev. 5:13)

NOTES

INTRODUCTION

1. Joseph Comblin, *The Meaning of Mission.* Trans. from Spanish, John Drury (Maryknoll, N.Y.: Orbis Books, 1977), p. 1.

2. Orlando E. Costas, *Theology of the Crossroads in Contemporary Latin America* (Amsterdam: Editions Rodopi, 1976), p. 328.

3. Some of the material in this chapter was used originally in the paper I delivered at the International Congress on World Evangelization in Lausanne, Switzerland, in 1974, and later published as "Depth in Evangelism —An Interpretation of 'In-Depth Evangelism' Around the World" in *Let the Earth Hear His Voice*, ed. J.D. Douglas (Minneapolis: World Wide Publications, 1975), pp. 675–94. It is used here with permission of World Wide Publications, Minneapolis, Minnesota.

CHAPTER I

1. Here we are confronted with two interrelated questions. There is, on the one hand, the importance of the written form of God's revelation. Granted, this form passes through human hands. Everything that is found in Scripture has been written by human beings. But why has it been written? To "instruct" us "for salvation through faith in Christ Jesus," says Paul (2 Tim. 3:14). And in this process of instructing for salvation, in the fulfillment of the prophetic and apostolic tasks (1 Pet. 2:9–10; 2 Cor. 5:20), the human authors of Scripture were "moved by the Holy Spirit" (2 Pet. 1:21). Their teaching, witness and proclamation were employed by God to convey his own Word. God uses the fulfillment of the prophetic and apostolic mission, the oral word, the word of the gospel (Rom. 10:14–18), to "breath" (*theopneustos*—2 Tim. 3:15) his own Word, "because the word of the prophets [and the apostles] is truly God's Word addressed to men" (G. C. Berkouwer, *Holy Scripture*, trans. Jack Rogers [Grand Rapids: Eerdmans, 1975], p. 146). The church is "built upon the foundation of

the apostles and prophets, Christ Jesus himself being the corner-
stone" (Eph. 2:20). Their word, being the initial proclamation of
the gospel, becomes the ground which the church's mission is
built. The church is the successor of the prophets and apostles.
But what makes this succession possible is the written text,
wherein God's Word, revealed through the prophetic and apostolic word, is faithfully transmitted. As Karl Barth has also
pointed out:

Everything depends for the idea of a living succession upon the
antecessor being thought of as still alive and possessed of free
power as compared with the *successor*. But this can only happen
when his proclamation is fixed in writing and when it is recognized that he still has life and free power to-day over the Church
in this very written Word of his. It is upon the written nature
of the canon, upon its character as *scriptura sacra*, that its auton-
omy and independence hang, and therefore its free power to-
wards the Church, and therefore the living nature of the succession. Of course it might also have pleased God to give His
Church the canon in the form of an unwritten prophetic and
apostolic tradition. . . . But . . . this [would leave] . . . the canon
. . . as faintly distinguishable from the life of the Church, as we
can distinguish the blood of our fathers which flows in our veins
from our own blood; in other words, the Church is once more
left to her solitary self and concentrated upon herself, upon her
own aliveness. Whatever such spiritual-oral tradition there may
be in the Church, obviously it cannot possess the character of an
authority irremovably confronting the Church, because it lacks
the written form. In the unwritten tradition the Church is not
addressed, but is engaged in a dialogue with herself. [Karl Barth,
Church Dogmatics I/1, trans. G. T. Thompson (Edinburgh: Clark,
1936), pp. 117–118.]

On the other hand, the biblical text is, still, a *human* word, even
though God-breathed. The fact that God employs the words of
the prophets and apostles for the transmission of his Word does
not exempt the Scriptures from historical conditioning. Indeed,
the fact that they are human makes them unique as vehicles of
God's revelation. God has chosen to make himself known in and
through human words. His revelation comes to us, therefore, as
part of human history.

   This means that Scripture, in order to be understood, must be
subject to the same scrutiny as is any human document. The
historical conditions under which it arose must be critically
analyzed in order for its message to be adequately interpreted.
Such a critical scrutiny affects not only the Scriptures as such,
but also our own use and interpretation of them, which suffer

from our own historical conditioning. The truth of faith is mediated by our respective sociohistorical contexts.

Precisely because the Bible is a book of faith, however, it must be interpreted in faith. It not only represents the historical witness of the community of faith but also presupposes an attitude of faith from its readers. Yet faith neither is an abstract body of truths nor a theoretical exercise. Faith is trust and commitment. In the words of Paul, it is obedience (Rom. 1:5). To read the Scriptures in faith is consequently to interpret them in obedience, in meditation and in engagement; it is not only to hear but also to do the Word (Jas. 1:22). Obedience, therefore, is the place from which the Word can be understood and where its truth can be verified.

For further discussions and various perspectives on the question of revelation and inspiration, including the authority of Scripture, see, among others: Berkouwer, *Scripture*, pp. 9ff., 240ff., 346ff.; Barth, *Dogmatics* I/1, pp. 51–283; Jack Rogers, ed., *Biblical Authority* (Waco, Texas: Word, 1977); Carl F. H. Henry, ed. *Revelation and the Bible* (Grand Rapids, Mich.: Baker Book House, 1958); James Barr, *The Bible in the Modern World* (London: SCM Press, 1973); Bernard Ramm, *Special Revelation and the Word of God* (Grand Rapids, Mich.: Eerdmans, 1961); and Luis Alonso Schokel, *La Palabra inspirada: La Biblia a la luz de la ciencia del lenguaje* (Barcelona: Biblioteca Herder, 1969).

On the hermeneutical question, see further, among others: E. Schillebeechx, *Interpretación de la Fe: Aportaciones a una Teología Hermenéutica y crítica*, trans. from German, José Mauleón (Salamanca: Ediciones Sígueme, 1973); Berkouwer, *Scripture*, pp. 213–239; Severino Croatto, *Liberación y libertad* (Buenos Aires: Ediciones Mundo Nuevo, 1973), pp. 11–146; H. M. Kuitert, *The Reality of Faith*, trans. Lewis B. Smedes (Grand Rapids, Mich.: Eerdmans, 1968), pp. 141–192; José Míguez-Bonino, *Doing Theology in a Revolutionary Situation* (Philadelphia: Fortress Press, 1975), pp. 86–105; Jerjes Ruiz, *Teología bíblica latinoamericana: Pautas hermenéuticas* (San José, Costa Rica: Seminario Bíblico Latinoamericano, 1977), pp. 40–112; and J. L. Segundo, *The Liberation of Theology*, trans. John Drury (Maryknoll, N.Y.: Orbis Books, 1976), pp, 7–182.

2. There is, however, a difference between the language used in reference to John and Jesus. While John is called an *angelon* (Matt. 11:10; Mk. 1:2; Lk. 7:27), Jesus is never designated thus. An *angelon* may be a heavenly or human messenger, but Jesus does not belong to the angelic category. On the contrary, his "sending" is related to the Father alone. It is as Son that Jesus is sent and not as an angelic figure or as an ordinary prophet. Hence, although John refuses to be identified with Elijah (Jn. 1:21), insist-

ing that Jesus is he (Matt. 11:3; 3:10–12), the words used for Jesus' mission are the verbs *appostellein* and *pempein*, both of which mean "to send" and refer to the divine origin and authority of his mission and to the Father's participation in the sending as such. Cf. Gerhard Kittel, "*angelos* in the NT," in *Theological Dictionary of the New Testament* (henceforth, *TDNT*), Vol. I, ed. by Gerhard Kittel, trans. and ed. Geoffrey W. Bromiley (Grand Rapids, Mich.: Eerdmans, 1969), pp. 13–87; Karl Heinrich Regstorf, "*apostello (pempo),*" in Kittel, pp. 398–406; C. U. Wolf, "Messenger," in *The Interpreter's Dictionary of the Bible*, Vol. K–Q, ed. George Arthur Buttrick (Nashville, Tenn.: Abingdon Press, 1962), pp. 359–360.

3. For an extensive treatment of the place of preaching in Jesus' ministry in the light of the four Gospels, see Robert H. Mounce, *The Essential Nature of New Testament Preaching* (Grand Rapids, Mich.: Eerdmans, 1960), pp. 28–51.

4. Cf. B. W. Anderson, "God, Name Of," in *Interpreter's Dictionary*, Vol. E–J, p. 408; Walther Eichrodt, *Theology of the Old Testament*, Vol. I, trans. J. A. Baker (London: SCM Press, 1961), pp. 173–174, 206ff., 409ff.

5. On the place of mission in the OT, see, among others, H. H. Rowley, *The Missionary Message of the Old Testament* (London: Carey Press, 1955); Johannes Blauw, *The Missionary Nature of the Church* (London: Lutterworth Press, 1972), pp. 15–54; Bengt Sundkler, *The World of Mission* (London: Lutterworth Press, 1965), pp. 11–17; R. Martin-Achard, *Israel et les nations—La perspective missionaire de l'Ancient Testament* (Neuchatel: Delachaux, 1959); Ives Raguin, *Théologie missionaire de l'Ancient Testament* (Paris: Editions du Seuil, 1947); J. Verkuyl, *Contemporary Missiology: An Introduction*, trans. Dale Cooper (Grand Rapids, Mich.: Eerdmans, 1978), pp. 90–100; Orlando E. Costas, ed., *Hacia una teología de la evangelización* (Buenos Aires: La Aurora, 1973), pp. 19–33.

6. I am indebted for these threefold designations to Juan Luis Segundo, *Our Idea of God*, Vol. III of *A Theology for Artisans of a New Humanity*, trans. John Drury (Maryknoll, N.Y.: Orbis Books, 1974), pp. 20–31.

7. The opposite is also true: Jesus of Nazareth not only reveals and represents God before women and men, but also reveals and represents humanity before God. In him, deity is incarnated and humanity divinized. In the words of Karl Barth,

In Jesus Christ there is no isolation of man from God or of God from man. . . . Jesus Christ is in His own Person, as true *God*, *man's* loyal partner, and as true *man*, *God's*. He is the Lord humbled for communion with man and likewise the Servant exalted to communion with God. . . . Thus He comes forward to *man* on behalf of *God* calling for an awakening faith, love, and hope, and to *God* on behalf of *man*, representing man, making satisfaction and interceding. Thus he attests and guarantees to man God's free *grace* and at the same time attests and guarantees to God man's free *gratitude*. Thus He establishes in His Person the justice of God *vis-à-vis* man and also the justice of man before God. [Karl Barth, *The Humanity of God*, trans. John Newton Thomas and Thomas Wieser (Atlanta: John Knox Press, 1960), pp. 46–47.]

8. National Council of the Churches of Christ in the U.S.A., "Evangelism Today," a policy statement adopted by the Board of Governors (March 3, 1976), p. 1.

9. Mortimer Arias, "That the World May Believe," *International Review of Mission*, 1976, *65* (257), 13–26.

10. Cf., among others, Rudolf Schnackenburg, *Reino y reinado de Dios: Estudio bíblico-teológico*, 2ud ed., trans. from the 4th German edition, José Gosgaya, OSA (Madrid: Ediciones Fax, 1970), pp. 239ff., 263ff.; John Bright, *The Kingdom of God: The Biblical Concept and Its Meaning for the Church* (Nashville: Abingdon Press, 1953), pp. 230ff.

11. Cf. James D. G. Dunn, *Jesus and the Spirit* (London: SCM Press, 1975), pp. 308ff.; Jürgen Moltmann, *The Church in the Power of the Spirit*, trans. Margaret Kohl (San Francisco: Harper & Row, 1975), pp. 33ff.

12. J. Verkuyl "The Mission of God and the Missions of the Churches," *Occasional Essays*, 1977, *4*(1), 40. Also in *Missiology*, p. 198.

13. Michael Green, "Methods and Strategy in the Evangelism of the Early Church," Part II, in *Let the Earth Hear*, p. 176.

14. Cf. Orlando E. Costas, "Conversion as a Complex Experience: A Personal Case Study," *Gospel in Context*, 1978, *1*(3), 14–24. Also in the same issue see Donald R. Jacobs, "Culture and the Phenomena of Conversion," pp. 4–13; various comments on both articles, pp. 25–34; and the responses of Jacobs and I, pp. 35–39.

15. Georg Bertram, *"Epistrepho,"* TDNT, Vol. VII, pp. 722–729.

16. William Barclay, *Turning to God: A Study of Conversion in the Book of Acts and Today* (Grand Rapids, Mich.: Baker Book House, 1972), pp. 21–22.

17. Bertram, *"Epistrepho,"* p. 727.

18. J. Behm, *"Metanoéo, Metanoia,"* TDNT, Vol. IV, pp. 980–982.

CHAPTER II

1. Cf. Juan Stam, "Bases Bíblicas para el Discipulado," *Ensayos Ocasionales*, 6 1976, *3*(1) 1–22, *passim*.

2. This pericope is part of the post-Easter sayings. It bears a close resemblance to Dan. 7:13–14 and follows in its structure the en-

thronement ceremony of the kings of the ancient Orient, which
was made up of three events: (1) exaltation, (2) presentation (or
proclamation) and (3) enthronement (transfer of power).

For Matthew, there is no need to mention the Ascension nor
Pentecost, inasmuch as Jesus continues to be present in history.
Jesus' death and resurrection have given way to his *exaltation,*
which in turn must be made *known* among all the peoples of the
earth, bringing them to obedience. This process will culminate
with the celebration of his enthronement. The purpose of discip-
ling the nations is to enable them to participate in the final
enthronment of Jesus Christ. "The one who has been given all
authority after his vicarious death on the cross is now in the
process of becoming Lord of all nations. Mission is therefore
both the consequence and the realization of his enthronement."
(Hans-Ruedi Weber, *The Invitation: Mathew On Mission* (New
York: Joint Commission on Education and Cultivation Board of
Missions of the United Methodist Church, 1971), pp. 94–95). In
this connection, it is significant to note the way Mathew uses the
word *all* (Gr. *panta*): all authority, all nations (Gr. *ethne,* "peoples"), all commands and all days.

Interestingly enough, Mathew does not refer to mission in the
way the other Synoptics do. For him, mission is but an extension
of Jesus' teaching ministry. Hence the stress on keeping the
commandments Jesus has given, on making disciples of the nations, on leading them to baptism and on teaching them to obey
him in all things. (Cf. O. Michel, "Menschensohn und Völker-
welt," *Evangelische Missions Zeitschrift,* 1941, pp. 257–267; J. Blauw,
Missionary Nature, pp. 83–89; Karl Barth, "An Exegetical Study of
Mathew 28: 16–20," trans. Thomas Wieser, in *The Theology of the
Christian Mission,* ed. Gerald H. Anderson (New York: McGraw-
Hill, 1961), pp. 55ff; Joachim Jeremias, *La promesa de Jesús para los
paganos,* trans. by José María Bernáldez from the German (Madrid: Ediciones Fax, 1974), pp. 52ff.); Ferdinand Hahn, *Mission in
the New Testament* (London: SCM Press, 1965), pp. 120ff.; Verkuyl,
Missiology, pp. 104ff.)

3. Dietrich Bonhoeffer, *The Cost of Discipleship,* 2nd ed., trans. R. H.
   Fuller (New York: Macmillan, 1963), pp. 45ff.
4. René Padilla, "Evangelism and the World," Part I, in *Let the
   Earth Hear,* pp. 126ff.
5. Segundo, *Liberation,* pp. 213ff.
6. David Moberg, *The Great Reversal: Evangelism versus Social Concern*
   (Philadelphia: Lippincott, 1972), p. 42.
7. Orlando E. Costas, "The USA: A Challenge for Third World
   Christians?" *Review and Expositor,* 1977, *74*(2), 191.
8. *Ibid.,* p. 192.
9. In the parable of the talents (Mt. 25:14–30) and in its Lukan

counterpart, the parable of the pounds (Lk. 19:11–27), faithfulness stands out as a fundamental trait of the life of the kingdom. Three servants are given proportionate responsibilities. Two are judged as faithful, one as unfaithful. The point of these two parables is not how much they were able to give back, but what they had done with the resources their Master had entrusted them with. The first two put their talents to work. They were neither afraid of their Master nor of the possibility of losing what they had been given and having nothing to give back. The third hid his talent in the ground. He was both afraid of the Master and of the future; consequently, he sought to "conserve" the little he had. As it turned out, however, it was the unafraid, the ones who set out to work without counting the cost, who were received into "the joy" (confidentiality) of their Master, not because they had now twice as much to give back, but because they had been *faithful* in their stewardship. They were able to render a good account of their resources and receive a positive reward for their work. The third was rejected and judged for his unfaithfulness. He lost, therefore, the little he had.

It is generally accepted that the Master in Matthew, and the Nobleman in Luke, represent Jesus Christ. But who are the servants? "In parables with three characters like this one, the spotlight falls, by the rule of 'end stress,' on the third character in the story—that is, on the servant." See A. M. Hunter, *Interpreting the Parables* (Philadelphia: Westminster Press, 1960), p. 81. From the context, it would seem as if this last servant represented in Jesus' mind the leaders of Israel, who, having been entrusted with God's revelation, hid it in their religious system and did not disseminate it. They will be called into accountability on the judgment day. (Cf. *Ibid.;* Joachim Jeremias, *Las parábolas de Jesús,* trans. from German, Francisco Javier Calvo (Estella, Spain: Editorial Verbo Divino, 1970), pp. 72ff.)

But the parables should also serve as a warning to the new members of the kingdom (the disciples) who have received the larger light of revelation. They are warned not to do what the leaders of Israel had done with God's treasure, but to be faithful in their stewardship of God's Word.

Conversely, it could be said that *true* servants (disciples) are characterized by their faithfulness to the cause of the kingdom. They are neither afraid of the future nor of the Lord who will come. They know that all that is expected of them is to be faithful in the trust they have been given.

10. In so doing, he stands in the line of the prophetic tradition of the OT, which was focused not on the ceremonies of the cult, but on the practice of justice (Jer. 22:13–16) and mercy (Hos. 6:6),

which are the only ways of verifying humility before God. This tradition is summarized in Mic. 6:8 and Deu. 10:12–13. It is continued by Jesus, who summarizes the law in the double commandment (Mk. 12:28); by Paul, for whom love represents the fullness of the law (Ro. 13:8–10) and who insists on the sacrifice of life as the basis of true worship (Ro. 12:1–2); by John the Apostle, for whom the true test of faith is justice and love (1 Jn. 3:7, 10); and by James, for whom true worship is defined in terms of kindness toward orphans and widows and righteous behavior (Jas. 1:27). Cf. Gerhard von Rad, *Teología de las tradiciones proféticas de Israel*, Vol. II of *Teología del Antiguo Testamento*, 2nd ed., trans. from German Luis Alsono Schokel (Salamanca: Ediciones Sígueme, 1973), pp. 231ff., 527; Eichrodt, *Old Testament*, Vol. II, pp. 327f.

11. This is the chief prince of Meshech, who in Ezek. 38–39 leads the evil forces that rise up against Yahweh. (Cf. C. B. Howie, "Gog and Magog," in *Interpreter's Dictionary*, Vol. E–J, pp. 436–437.

12. Lane, *Mark*, pp. 67–68.

13. Carl Braaten, "The Christian Mission and American Imperialism," in *Religion and the Dilemmas of Nationhood*, ed. Sydney E. Ahlstrom (Minneapolis: Lutheran Church in America, 1976), p. 71.

14. Luke's narrative mixes material apparently gathered from other instances in the ministry of Jesus and even from various sources. To be sure, it parallels Mark's version, but it has many elements that do not appear in the latter. It has many similarities with the postresurrection incident recorded in Jn. 21:1–11, but also many differences.

Luke, like Mark, has his own theological reasons for constructing the narrative the way he does. For one thing, he emphasizes the miracles, thereby setting the call in the context of Jesus' mighty deeds. He also stresses Jesus' teaching ministry, Peter's role as a senior partner of John and James and, especially, the importance of obedience in the call to discipleship. (Cf., among others, Carroll Stuhlmaueller, C.P., "Evangelio según Lucas," *Comentario bíblico "San Jerónimo,"* ed. Raymond E. Brown, SS, Joseph A. Fitzmeyer, SJ, and Roland E. Murphy, O. Carm.; trans. Alfonso de la Fuente Adanez, Jesús Valiente Malla and Juan José del Moral from the English (Madrid: Ediciones Cristiandad, 1972), pp. 340–341; Hans Conzelmann, *El centro del tiempo: La teología de Lucas*, trans. from the 5th German ed., José María Bernáldez Montalvo (Madrid: Ediciones Fax, 1974), pp. 68–69; and I. Howard Marshall, *The Gospel of Luke: A Commentary on the Greek Text: The New International Greek Testament Commentary* (Exeter, England: Patermoster Press, 1978), pp. 199–206.)

15. John Stott, "Obeying Christ in a Changing World," in *The Lord*

Christ, Vol. I of *Obeying Christ in a Changing World,* ed. John Stott (Glasgow: Collins.

16. Bonhoeffer, *Discipleship,* p. 46.

CHAPTER III

1. R. Kenneth Strachan, "Call to Witness," *International Review of Mission,* 1964, *53* (210), 191–200.
2. On the relationship of 1 Pet. 2:9–10 to the church's mission, see Blauw, *Missionary Nature,* pp. 126ff.
3. This implies not only faithfulness to the norm of Scripture, but also discernment of the church's vital situation. (Cf., among others, Berkouwer, *Scripture,* pp. 327–345; Karl Barth, *La proclamación del evangelio,* trans. from French, Francisco Báez (Salamanca: Ediciones Sígueme, 1969), pp. 13–71; Edmund P. Clowney, *Preaching and Biblical Theology* (Grand Rapids, Mich.: Eerdmans, 1961); John Knox, *The Integrity of Preaching* (Nashville, Tenn: Abingdon Press, 1967); Luis Maldonado, *El menester de la predicación* (Salamanca: Ediciones Sígueme, 1972); Gardner Taylor, *How Shall They Preach: The Lyman Beecher Lectures and Five Sermons* (Elgin, Ill.: Progressive Baptist Publishing House, 1977); Clyde E. Fant, *Bonhoeffer: Wordly Preaching* (Nashville, Tenn.: Nelson, 1975).
4. Dietrich Bonhoeffer, *No Rusty Swords* (New York: Harper & Row, 1965), p. 20.
5. Jean-Jacques von Allmen, *Preaching and Congregation* (Richmond, Va.: John Knox Press, 1962), p. 31.

CHAPTER IV

1. Emil Brunner, *The Word and the World* (London: SCM Press, 1931), p. 108.
2. C. Peter Wagner, *Frontiers in Mission Strategy* (Chicago: Moody Press, 1971).
3. Paul Pretiz, "Cuenca, Ecuador: Two Years Later," *In-Depth Evangelism Around the World,* 1973, *1* (2), 22–23, 26–30.
4. *Ibid.*
5. *Ibid.,* pp. 29, 30.
6. Iglesia Episcopal de Ecuador, "Estado general de las misiones al 31 de diciembre de 1976 con proyección a 1977," Quito, 1977. Mimeographed.
7. Max Warren, *I Believe in the Great Commission* (Grand Rapids, Mich.: Eerdmans, 1976), p. 178.
8. Cf. H. Richard Niebuhr, *The Social Sources of Denominationalism* (Cleveland: World Publishing, 1929).

9. This is certainly the best rendering of the word *knowledge* (Gr. *epignoseous*) in Eph. 4:13. It refers to a personal rather than an intellectual knowledge. Cf. William F. Arndt and F. Wilbur Gingrich, *A Greek-English Lexicon of the New Testament and Other Early Christian Literature* (Chicago: University of Chicago Press, 1957), p. 291. In Eph. 1:17, the word is used in a similar way, and in Eph. 3:19 there is an even more forceful reference to the knowledge of Christ as a personal experience.

10. For a detailed treatment of Eph. 4:12 and the arguments that support the particular interpretation I am following, see Markus Barth, *Ephesians: Translation and Commentary on Chapters 4–6, The Anchor Bible* (New York: Doubleday, 1974), pp. 477–479.

11. On the biblical conception of light and darkness, see, among others, F. Baudraz, "Luz," *Vocabulario bíblico,* ed. by Jean-Jacques von Allmen, trans. José María González Ruiz from the French (Madrid: Marova, 1973), pp. 185–186; André Feuillet and Pierre Grelot, "Luz," *Vocabulario de teología bíblica,* ed. Xavier León Dufour, trans. from French, Alejandro Ros (Barcelona: Editorial Herder, 1967), pp. 821–825; and O. A. Piper, "Light, Light and Darkness," *Interpreter's Dictionary,* Vol. K–Q, pp. 130–132.

12. On the notion of the church as the eschatological pilgrim people of God, see Jurgen Moltmann, *Theology of Hope,* trans. from German, James W. Leitch (New York: Harper & Row, 1967), pp. 304–338.

13. This should not be construed as an escape into a non-worldly reality. To say that the Christian hope lies in the city that is yet to come is to underscore the fact that for Christians no human achievement, and therefore no sociopolitical project, is an ultimate. It is to affirm the "eschatological reserve" with which Christians enter into the human struggle for justice and liberation and the transcendent source (God) of their motivation. It is precisely the hope in a world that is yet to come, the new heaven and the new earth (Rev. 21:1) that is given to humankind in Jesus Christ, that frees Christians to participate creatively and critically in the struggle for justice and liberation. It enables Christians, on the one hand, to denounce situation of injustice, to become critical of the *status quo,* to refuse to conform to the present. On the other hand, it pushes them to look for a better tomorrow, to envision a society where justice, peace and community are not mere ideals but factual realities, to participate in the coming into being of a radically new world. As Gustavo Gutiérrez has said:

Christian hope opens us, in an attitude of spiritual childhood, to the gift of the future promised by God. It keeps us from any confusion of the Kingdom with any one historical stage, from any idolatry toward unavoidably ambiguous human achievement, from any absolutizing of revolution. In this way hope makes us radically free to commit ourselves to social praxis, motivated by a liberating utopia and with the means which the scientific analysis of reality provides for us. And our hope not only frees us for this commitment; it simultaneously demands and judges it.

[Gustavo Gutiérrez, *A Theology of Liberation*, trans. and ed. Sister Caridad Inda and John Eagleson (Maryknoll, N.Y.: Orbis Books, 1973), p. 238.]

14. Cf. Rubem Alves, *Theology of Human Hope* (Washington, D.C.: Corpus Publications, 1969), pp. 87ff.

15. Herein lies what could be called a fourth complementary aspect of church growth. As *breadth* has been linked to numerical expansion, *depth* to conceptual, experiential and organic development and *height* to the enrichment and refinement of our Christian lifestyles, so *length* can be associated with hope. The church should grow in the vision of its own future and in its commitment to God's coming kingdom. This will keep it, on the one hand, from false messianisms and triumphalistic attitudes and, on the other, from nihilistic pessimisms and a defeatist, inferiority complex.

16. Cf. J. C. Hoekendijk, *The Church Inside Out*, ed. L. A. Hoedemaker and Pieter Tijmes; trans. from Dutch, Isaac Rottenberg (Philadelphia: Westminster Press, 1964).

CHAPTER V

1. World Conference on Church and Society, *Christians in the Technical and Social Revolutions of our Time* (Geneva: World Council of Churches, 1967), p. 141.

2. H. H. Paul VI, *"Populorum Progressio,"* *Ocho grandes mensajes*, ed. Jesús Iribarren y José Luis Gutiérrez García (Madrid: Biblioteca de Autores Cristianos, 1971), p. 361.

3. Commission on the Churches' Participation in Development, *To Break the Chains of Oppression* (Geneva: World Council of Churches, 1975), p. 4.

4. *Ibid.*, p. 5.

5. *Ibid.*, p. 6.

6. *Ibid.*, p. 7.

7. Gutiérrez, *Liberation*, p. 37.

8. Cf. André Trocmé, *Jesus and the Nonviolent Revolution*, trans. Michael H. Shank and Marlin E. Miller (Scottdale, Pa.: Herald Press, 1963), pp. 19–76; John Howard Yoder, *The Politics of Jesus* (Grand Rapids, Mich.: Eerdmans, 1972), pp. 64–77.

9. On the concept of poverty in the OT, see Agustin George, "La

pobreza en el Antiguo Testamento," *La pobreza evangélica hoy*, trans. Hermanas Soledad Charria y Gloria Atuesta, o.p., from the French (Bogotá: Secretariado General de la CLAR, 1971), pp. 11–26; and Tomás Hanks, "La opresión y la pobreza en la teología bíblica" (San José: Minamundo, 1978), pp. 2–20 (Mimeographed). For the NT, see also the latter, pp. 21–31; Jacques Dupont, "Los pobres y la pobreza en los Evangelios y en los Hechos," *Pobreza evangélica*, pp. 27–44; Philip Seidensticker, "San Pablo y la pobreza," *Ibid.*, pp. 63–89; Béda Rigaux, "El radicalismo del reino," *Ibid.*, pp. 91–115; Richard Batey, *Jesus and the Poor: The Poverty Program of the First Christians* (New York: Harper & Row, 1972); and Herman Ridderbos, *The Coming of the Kingdom*, trans. H. de Jongsts, ed. Raymond O. Zorn (Philadelphia: Presbyterian and Reformed Publishing, 1975), pp. 185–191. For the place of the poor in both testaments, see Richard Bammel, *"Ptochos," TDNT*, Vol. VI, pp. 885–915; Julio de Santa Ana, *El desafío de los pobres a la iglesia*, Colección DEI (San José Costa Rica: Editorial Universitaria Centroamericana, 1977), pp. 17–71; and Tomás Hanks, "Pobreza," *Diccionario de la Biblia*, pp. 516–517.

10. For further discussion on the poor, see the Excursus following this chapter.

11. Cf. Claus Westermann, *Isaiah 40–66: A Commentary* (Philadelphia: Westminster Press, 1969), pp. 331–342; Thomas Hanks, "Isaiah 58 and the Year of Jubilee," unpublished article, pp. 1–13.

12. Cf. Yoder, *Politics*, pp. 66–74.

13. *Ibid.*, p. 66.

EXCURSUS

1. De Santa Ana, *Los Pobres*, p. 5.
2. *Ibid.*, p. 8.
3. Ridderbos, *Kingdom*, p. 189.
4. Bammel, *"Ptochos," TDNT*, Vol. III, p. 905.
5. Orlando E. Costas, "Propositions," *separata* of *Theology of the Crossroads in Contemporary Latin America (Academisch Proefschrift, Vrije Universiteit te Amsterdam*, 2 april 1976).
6. G. D. Gort, "Gospel for the Poor?" In *Zending op Weg Naar de Toekomst: Essays Aangeboden aan Prof. Dr. J. Verkuyl* (Kampen, The Netherlands: Kok, 1978), p. 89. Hereafter all references to this work shall be noted in the text itself.
7. By inference, because Gort claims that his use of the proposition is *"solely* as a useful paradigmatic statement" and is not meant to be a criticism of my theological position (p. 89). But is it possible to separate (as Gort proposes) an author from his works, or his theology from statements like the proposition in question, espe-

cially when the author has defended it, insisting that it *is* consistent with his theological stance?

8. Cf. Hanks, "La opresión y la pobreza," pp. 2ff.

9. On the implications of oppression for oppressors and their need for liberation, see the excellent article by Jurgen Moltmann and M. Douglas Meeks, "The Liberation of Oppressors," *Christianity and Crisis*, 1978, *38*(20), 310–317.

10. For a thorough exposition of this problem in biblical literature, see José Porfirio Miranda, *Marx and the Bible*, trans. John Eagleson (Maryknoll, N.Y.: Orbis Books, 1974).

11. Moltmann, *Crucified God*, pp. 291–340.

12. Orlando E. Costas, "Mission out of Affluence," *Missiology*, 1973, *1*(4), 413.

13. Gutiérrez, *Liberation*, p. 302.

CHAPTER VI

1. For an ample discussion of the political context of Revelation, with numerous references, see Juan Stam, "El Apocalipsis y el Imperialismo," *Capitalismo: violencia y anti-vida*, Tomo I, ed. Elsa Tamez and Saul Trinidad (San José Costa Rica: Editorial Universitaria Centroamericana, 1978), pp. 359ff.

2. George Eldon Ladd, *A Commentary on the Revelation of John* (Grand Rapids, Mich.: Eerdmans, 1972), p. 73.

3. Alfred Lapple, *El Apocalipsis de San Juan: Un libro vital del cristianismo*, trans. from German, Alejo Oria León (Madrid: Ediciones Paulinas, 1971), p. 102.

4. José Comblin, *Cristo en el Apocalipsis*, trans. from French, Alejandro Esteban Latos Ros (Barcelona: Editorial Herder, 1969), p. 32.

5. Lapple, *Apocalipsis*, p. 101.

6. *Ibid.*, p. 102.

7. Ladd, *Revelation*, p. 75.

8. *Ibid.*

9. León Morris, *Revelation. Tyndale New Testament Commentaries* (Grand Rapids, Mich.: Eerdmans, 1970), p. 91.

10. Cf. Costas, *The Church*, pp. 37–44.

11. Moltmann, *Crucified God*, p. 73.

12. The image depicted in Heb. 13:12–13 is taken from the OT sacrifices (Lev. 16:2–28). On the Day of Atonement, the High Priest would take two goats, one to be presented to the Lord as a sin offering, the other to be sent away into the wilderness with the sins of the people. However, the goat presented as a sin offering, along with the bull that the High Priest offered for himself, had to be carried outside the camp once the offering had been made.

There "their skin and their flesh and their dung" had to be burned (Lev. 16:27).

It seems to me that Hebrews changes the image of the two goats into a single person: Jesus Christ. He took on himself the sins of the people, suffering outside the gate in order to sanctify them through his own blood (Heb. 13:12). The fact that the sacrifice took place outside the camp (in the unsanctified ground, where both the "scapegoat" was sent and the sacrificed goat was burned), demonstrates that, according to the author of Hebrews, Jesus died in the place where the outcast found their dwellings. He could only redeem a sinful world by dying in its midst and taking on himself their sins. Christ's sacrifice was far superior to the sacrifice of the Day of Atonement. It also shifted the locus of God's redemptive action—from the close circle of the Jewish Commonwealth to the open space of an alienated world. This open space has become the sphere of the church's mission (Heb. 13:13).

SELECTED BIBLIOGRAPHY

The following books represent additional relevant material on the inner life and outreach of the church. Works cited in the footnotes have been omitted from this bibliography, and only current books in English have been included.

Adams, Arthur M.
 1970 *Administration in the Church*. Philadelphia: United Presbyterian Church in the USA.
Alves, Rubem
 1969 *Theology of Human Hope*. Washington, D.C.: Corpus Books.
 1972 *Tomorrow's Child*. New York: Harper & Row.
Anderson, Gerald, and Stransky, Thomas F., ed.
 1974 *Mission Trends No. 1: Crucial Issues in Missions Today*. New York: Paulist Press.
 1975 *Mission Trends No. 2: Evangelization*. New York: Paulist Press.
 1977 *Mission Trends No. 3: Third World Theologies*. New York: Paulist Press.
 1979 *Mission Trends No. 4: Liberation Theologies in North America and Europe*. New York: Paulist Press.
Beaver, Pierce R., ed.
 1977 *American Missions in Bicentennial Perspective*. South Pasadena, Calif.: William Carey Library.
Boberg, John T., S.V.D., and Scherer, James, ed.
 1972 *Mission in the 70's*. Chicago: Cluster of Theological Schools.
Boff, Leonardo
 1978 *Jesus Christ Liberator*. Trans. John Drury. Maryknoll, N.Y.: Orbis Books.
Borchert, Gerald L.
 1976 *Dynamics of Evangelism*. Fort Worth, Texas: Word Books.
Braaten, Carl E.
 1977 *The Flaming Center: A Theology of the Christian Mission*. Philadelphia: Fortress Press.
Brown, Robert McAfee
 1978 *Theology in a New Key: Responding to Liberation Themes*. Philadelphia: Westminster Press.
Bühlmann, Walbert
 1976 *The Coming of the Third Church: An Analysis of the Present and Future of the Church*. London: St. Paul Publications.

Castro, Emilio
1975 *Amidst Revolution.* Belfast: Christian Journals.
Danker, William J., and Kang, Wi Jo, ed.
1971 *The Future of the Christian World Mission.* Grand Rapids, Mich.: Eerdmans.
De Santa Ana, Julio, ed.
1978 *Separation Without Hope? Essays on the Relation Between the Church and the Poor During the Industrial Revolution and the Western Colonial Expansion.* Geneva: Commission on the Churches' Participation in Development, World Council of Churches.
Douglas, J. D., ed.
1975 *Let the Earth Hear His Voice: International Congress on World Evangelization.* Minneapolis: World Wide Publications.
Drummond, Louis A.
1972 *Leading Your Church in Evangelism.* Nashville, Tenn.: Broadman Press.
Dubose, Francis M.
1978 *How Churches Grow in an Urban World.* Nashville, Tenn.: Broadman Press.
Dussel, Enrique
1976 *History and the Theology of Liberation.* Trans. John Drury. Maryknoll, N.Y.: Orbis Books.
Ellacuria, Ignacio
1976 *Freedom Made Flesh: The Mission of Christ and His Church.* Trans. John Drury. Maryknoll, N.Y.: Orbis Books.
Engel, James F., and Norton, Wilbert
1975 *What's Gone Wrong with the Harvest?* Grand Rapids, Mich.: Zondervan Corporation.
Escobar, Samuel, and Driver, John
1978 *Christian Mission and Social Justice.* Scottdale, Pa.: Herald Press.
Fackre, Gabriel
1975 *Word in Deed: Theological Themes in Evangelism.* Grand Rapids, Mich.: Eerdmans.
1978 *The Christian Story: A Narrative Interpretation of Basic Christian Doctrine.* Grand Rapids, Mich.: Eerdmans.
Fraser, Ian
1975 *The Fire Runs.* London: SCM Press.
Gilmore, Alec
1975 *Tomorrow's Pulpit.* London: Lutterworth Press.
Goulet, Denis
1974 *A New Moral Order: Studies in Development Ethics and Liberation Theology.* Maryknoll, N.Y.: Orbis Books.
Gray, Robert N.
1976 *Managing the Church.* Vol. I: *Church Business Administration.* Enid, Okla.: Haymaker Press.

Gutierrez, Gustavo, and Shaull, Richard
   1977 *Liberation and Change.* Atlanta: John Knox Press.
Hamid, Idris, ed.
   1977 *Out of the Depths.* San Fernando, Trinidad: St. Andrew's
   Theological College.
Hayward, Victor
   1974 *Christians and China.* Belfast: Christian Journals.
   1974 *China Today.* Birmingham: Selly Oak Colleges.
Hebly, J. A.
   1978 *The Russians and the World Council of Churches.* Belfast: Christian Journals Limited.
Hendrick, John R.
   1977 *Opening the Door of Faith.* Atlanta: John Knox Press.
Holmes, Lionel, ed.
   1978 *Church and Nationhood.* New Delhi: Theological Commission of the World Evangelical Fellowship.
Hopkins, Paul A.
   1977 *What Next in Mission?* Philadelphia: Westminster Press.
IDOC
   1973 *An Asian Theology of Liberation. No. 5: The Philippines.* New York: IDOC International.
   1974 *The Future of the Missionary Enterprise. No. 9: In Search of Mission.* New York: IDOC International.
   1976 *The Future of the Missionary Enterprise. No. 17: Mission in America in World Context.* New York: IDOC International.
   1978 *The Future of the Missionary Enterprise. No. 19: Mission Within African Societies.* New York: IDOC International.
Kelly, Dean M.
   1977 *Why Conservative Churches Are Growing.* 2nd ed. San Francisco: Harper & Row.
Koyama, Kosuke
   1977 *No Handle on the Cross: An Asian Meditation on the Crucified Mind.* Maryknoll, N.Y.: Orbis Books.
Kraft, Charles H.
   1979 *Christianity in Culture.* Maryknoll, N.Y.: Orbis Books.
Krass, Alfred C.
   1974 *Go . . . And Make Disciples.* London: S.P.C.K.
   1978 *Five Lanterns at Sundown: Evangelism in a Chastened Mood.* Grand Rapids, Mich.: Eerdmans.
Lausanne Theology and Education Group
   1978 "The Pasadena Consultation—Homogeneous Unit." *Lausanne Occasional Papers No. 1.* Wheaton: Lausanne Committee for World Evangelization.
   1978 "The Willowbank Report—Gospel and Culture." *Lausanne Occasional Papers No. 2.* Wheaton, Illinois: Lausanne Committee for World Evangelization.

Lindgren, Alvin J.
1965 *Foundations for Purposeful Church Administration.* Nashville, Tenn.: Abingdon Press.

Míguez-Bonino, José
1976 *Christians and Marxists: The Mutual Challenge to Revolution.* London: Hodder and Stoughton.

Miranda, José Porfirio
1974 *Marx and the Bible: A Critique of the Philosophy of Oppression.* Trans. John Eagleson. Maryknoll, N.Y.: Orbis Books.
1977 *Being and the Messiah: The Message of St. John.* Trans. John Drury. Maryknoll, N.Y.: Orbis Books.

Moltmann, Jurgen
1978 *The Open Church: Invitation to a Messianic Lifestyle.* London: SCM Press.

Newbigin, Leslie
1977 *The Good Shepherd: Meditations on Christian Ministry in Today's World.* Grand Rapids, Mich.: Eerdmans.
1978 *The Open Secret: Sketches for a Missionary Theology.* Grand Rapids, Mich.: Eerdmans.

Padilla, C. René, ed.
1976 *The New Face of Evangelicalism: A Symposium on the Lausanne Covenant.* London: Hodder and Stoughton.

Reilly, Michael Collin, S.J.
1978 *Spirituality for Mission: Historical, Theological and Cultural Factors for a Present-Day Missionary Spirituality.* New York: Orbis Books.

Richardson, Don
1974 *Peace Child.* Glendale, Calif.: G/L Regal Books.

Schaller, Lyle E.
1971 *Parish Planning: How to Get Things Done in Your Church.* Nashville, Tenn.: Abingdon Press.

Segundo, Juan Luis
1972–74 *A Theology for Artisans of a New Humanity.* 5 vols. Trans. John Drury. Maryknoll, N.Y: Orbis Books.

Shelley, Marshall, ed.
1978 *Unreached Peoples '79.* Elgin, Ill.: Cook.

Sider, Ronald
1977 *Rich Christians in an Age of Hunger.* Downers Grove, Ill.: Inter-Varsity Press.

Snyder, Howard A.
1975 *The Problem of Wine Skins: Church Structures in a Technological Age.* Downers Grove, Ill.: Inter-Varsity Press.
1977 *The Community of the King.* Downers Grove, Ill.: Inter-Varsity Press.

Song, Choan-Seng
1977 *Christian Mission in Reconstruction—An Asian Analysis.* Maryknoll, N.Y.: Orbis Books.

Strachan, R. Kenneth
1968 *The Inescapable Calling.* Grand Rapids, Mich.: Eerdmans.
Sweazey, George E.
1978 *The Church as Evangelist.* San Francisco: Harper & Row.
Taylor, John V.
1975 *Enough Is Enough.* London: SCM Press.
Thomas, William
1977 *An Assessment of Mass Meetings as a Method of Evangelism: A Case Study on Eurofest.* Amsterdam: Editions Rodopi.
Torres, Sergio, and Fabella, Virginia, ed.
1978 *The Emergent Gospel: Theology from the Underside of History.* Maryknoll, N.Y.: Orbis Books.
Various
1975 *Evangelism: Mandates for Action.* New York: Hawthorn Books.
1978 *Church and State: Opening a New Ecumenical Discussion.* Geneva: World Council of Churches.
Verkuyl, Johannes
1970 *The Message of Liberation in Our Age.* Grand Rapids, Mich.: Eerdmans.
Verkuyl, Johannes, and Nordholt, H. G. Schulte
1974 *Responsible Revolution: Means and Ends for Transforming Society.* Grand Rapids, Mich.: Eerdmans.
Wagner, Peter
1979 *Our Kind of People: The Ethical Dimensions of Church Growth in America.* Atlanta: John Knox Press.
Wallis, Jim
1976 *Agenda for Biblical People.* San Francisco: Harper & Row.
Watson, David
1976 *I Believe in Evangelism.* Grand Rapids, Mich.: Eerdmans.
Weingartner, Erich, ed.
1976 *Church Within Socialism: Church and State in East European Socialist Republics.* Rome: IDOC International.
Wong, James, Larson, Peter, and Pentecost, Edward
1973 *Missions from the Third World.* Singapore: Church Growth Study Center.

INDEX